The Cave

CLARK COOLIDGE

BERNADETTE MAYER

ADVENTURES IN POETRY

Cover photograph of Eldon's Cave by Kevin Downey
Book design by *typeslowly*

Printed in Michigan by Cushing-Malloy, Inc.
on Glatfelter Natures Recycled paper

Adventures in Poetry titles are distributed to the trade through Zephyr Press
by Consortium Book Sales and Distribution [www.cbsd.com]
& SPD [www.spdbooks.org]

9 8 7 6 5 4 3 2 FIRST PRINTING IN 2009

www.adventuresinpoetry.com

Contents

AN INTRODUCTION TO *THE CAVE*–Marcella Durand

Clark Coolidge and Bernadette Mayer began writing *The Cave* nine days after they took a trip on September 10, 1972, to Eldon's Cave in Massachusetts. Eldon's Cave is located in West Stockbridge and Coolidge had first visited it with his father when he was 12 years old. He describes it as small, damp, and at first "awful looking." But at some point, the cave opens up–and in fact looks surprisingly striking, with waves of banded marble, in the occasional photo from out-of-print books in Coolidge's collection. The party of 1972 consisted of Coolidge, Mayer, filmmaker Ed Bowes (at the time Mayer's boyfriend), and Susan and Celia Coolidge.

The group never made it into the larger area of the cave, for a number of reasons. In fact, recountings of the trip, which seems to have started out as just something to do during a visit to the Coolidges, include a number of contradictions. Bowes got soaked early on in the cave and wanted to turn back. Then it turns out that Mayer never actually went inside. Instead, at the cave's entrance, she got her period–a heavy one. She says at that moment it seemed "absolutely terrifying to go into the cave." Later, Coolidge uncovered information about women in the 19th century suffering excessive menstrual flow upon entering Mammoth Cave in Kentucky, which he says he and Bernadette discussed "with interest." Both of them actually seem, post-Cave, fascinated with the menstruation–it seems to have functioned as a sort of disruption or omission, a fruitfully troubling "spot in time" (*sic*) in a spelunk that Coolidge otherwise describes as a "non-event" and even "kind of a bust."

From such a seemingly mundane beginning grew an extraordinary document, a palimpsest of a moment in literary history. *The Cave* documents, in an unusually transparent way, the meeting of minds between two of the most innovative and original writers of the late 20th century. It also accompanied an extraordinary period of writing for Coolidge and Mayer, during which both writers were pushing the limits of how far they could write. Around and after *The Cave* were expansive, seemingly endless public readings, and the genesis of other major works, such as *Memory* and *Studying Hunger* (Mayer) and *The Maintains* and an as-yet-unpublished long prose work (Coolidge) (of which several pages are actually a take on the grids of photos for Mayer's *Memory* installation). "We were all interested in writing thousands of pages every day," says Coolidge. "A feeling of everything being kept on forever . . . we didn't understand endings," although Mayer says, of why *The Cave* ended when it did, with the final installment dated June 1978, "Everything comes to an end for a writer. It couldn't go on forever."

Coolidge remembers Mayer suggesting that he write down a straight account of everything that happened the day they visited Eldon's Cave, and that they begin collaborating from it. From this account, titled appropriately enough "The Trip to Eldon's Cave," the collaboration quickly took shape. *The Cave* is written in prose, in verse, in dialogue—and also functions as a breathtakingly fast call-and-response between Mayer and Coolidge. Words, characters, and themes are picked up in each subsequent contribution and quickly torqued into something else, some new point of departure. Literary and historical characters (Herman Melville, Nathaniel, Sophia, Julian and Una Hawthorne, Louis Malle, Samuel Beckett, Floyd Collins,[1] and Julie Harris,[2] who reportedly owned Eldon's Cave) have what one would today call "mind-warpy" conversations with each other. Mayer was a fan of Hawthorne and Coolidge a fan of Melville, and Mayer and Coolidge would talk to each other as if they were Hawthorne and Melville: *The Cave* continues this private theater in print, providing public form to these writers' conversations and improvisations.

The poetic expansion and compression of *The Cave* is stunning, evidence of Coolidge and Mayer's enormous range of intake—John McPhee, Guy Davenport, geology, science, dictionaries, thesauruses, music, conceptual art, film. Coolidge describes a series of three "really quite gorgeous" videos that Ed Bowes made, documenting this interplay of influence. The first video, shot in Coolidge's house in Hancock, MA, depicted Coolidge and Mayer reading from the Yale Gertrude Stein. Another was of Mayer and Coolidge reading "The Maintains" and "Studying Hunger" in Mayer and Bowes's loft on Grand Street in Manhattan. The third required Coolidge and Mayer to read and move continuously—as Coolidge read from the thesaurus and Mayer read from the dictionary, they got tangled up in wires. According to Coolidge, these films were shown (in lieu of a reading) at the Poetry Project at St. Mark's. Yet, excruciatingly, tantalizingly, no one seems to know where the films are now, and the Poetry Project's records of the event are, at best, sketchy. And speaking of film, Coolidge clearly remembers Bowes filming their trip into Eldon's Cave, but the film itself is elusive. Was it actually shot? Mayer says "If Ed didn't bring any camera equipment, then Eldon's Cave was not a real cave." What happened to that film of the trip into Eldon's Cave is yet another mystery among a Rashomon-like group recollection of the event.

---

[1] Floyd Collins was a 1920s spelunker who was trying to link his Crystal Cave to Sand Cave, which had an entrance closer to the main highway, in the hopes of attracting more tourists. Unfortunately, during his efforts a rock trapped his foot (and therefore Collins), leading to a full-on rescue attempt in 1925 that, alas, failed.

[2] Actually, more accurately, it's Julie Harris's breasts who make appearances in *The Cave*, which may lend insight into Mayer's scrawled "MEN WITH BREASTS," as well as other breast references in the collaboration. As I recall, we thought it was funny to seem sexually fixated on the breasts of an actress who was hardly known as a 'sex star,'" says Coolidge.

Tracking the title of "The Cave," or more accurately, the titles, is another intriguing process. Ange Mlinko gave me a copy of *The Cave* along with a note from Coolidge that somewhat mystifying says, "Maybe we should have just titled it 'THE CAVE'?" But on the copy itself, it says "The Cave Work" (along with "CONCLAVE/ECHOS/BREASTS" jotted on the bottom). In a letter dated September 9, 1994, not long before Mayer and Coolidge ceased their correspondence altogether, Mayer writes "I remember when we talked about calling it 'Clark's Nipples'—that was probably around the time we were encouraging you to call everything you wrote 'My Penis.'" She also adds that an "enticing" title would be "The Clark's Nipples of what a wreckage corrects." Another title that occasionally crops up in their correspondence is "Cave of Metonymy," which is also the title of one of the longer sections. Today, in more prosaic times perhaps, Mayer calls it the "Cave Collaboration" (or CC, which can also refer to Coolidge).

The order of the sections of *The Cave* (which seems to be the present title, by general consensus) also changed over the years. In the same 1994 letter, Mayer lists *The Cave*'s contents: the beginning "The Body of Water with the Bowl," a two-page poem that Clark wrote three days after the trip, "by eyeballing a text on Eldon's Cave that I had in a book on New England caves," was thrown out for not actually being part of the collaboration, and "also because we wanted to start with the straight account," says Coolidge. Mayer also includes some notes on *The Cave*, which refer to *The Aeneid* and "Inferno," and back to caves themselves, as well as their surroundings: "Rocks, caves, lakes, fens, bogs, dens, & shades of death." The notes disintegrate (or integrate, depending on how one sees it) into a scrawl: "Tom Balls/ MEN WITH BREASTS/ Marbles/ HELL/ this our pinching cave/ A ROCK is NOT a word/ The host/ LUCKy-CAVE/ Passage/ CAVE/ CLEAN VASE/ Conclave/CON-CLAVE." Maybe this illuminates, or at least ECHOES "CONCLAVE/ECHOS/BREASTS."

Like all load-bearing construction, *The Cave* reveals how the two writers were taking apart language and reassembling it into something brand-new. But *The Cave* also seems incomplete—on finishing "Let's just stop . . . ," the final poem in the collaboration, one wants more, despite Mayer's feeling that it couldn't go on forever. Compared to the expansiveness of the two writers' other works at the time, it is frustratingly truncated. But it is also accessible: it begins from concreteness, a specific event that is quickly revealed to be as slippery as memory, with the bitternesses and contradictions and murkiness of the time taking over. Mayer emphasizes that *The Cave* had nothing to do with the symbolic nature of caves. Rather, *The Cave* is meant to be real, here, in the words and art and thoughts of today. The rawness and roughness of *The Cave* is also exactly what makes it valuable—essential reading for anyone who wants to investigate the development of innovative writing in the 1970s, 80s, 90s, and beyond.

THE CAVE

THE TRIP TO ELDON'S CAVE–Sunday Sept. 10, 1972

Sunday afternoon. We pack up in the car. Ed Bernadette Susan Celia & CC.
Drive down thru Richmond, West Stockbridge, cross the turnpike, Williamsville.
Turn right on dirt road a little ways. The gap in the meadow stonewall I remember
from lots of other times here. This time there's a big new white sign says CAVE
CLOSED TO PUBLIC/NO TRESPASSING. Last year there was just a little weathered
flapsign on tree opposite meadow with arrow pointing in, CAVE. What to do?
Consternation pissed-off & hmmm. Drive down to end of dirtroad turnaround
& start knocking on doors find the new owner. Guess Julie Harris sold it to new
landgrubber, probly doesn't even live around here. Nobody home. Try next house.
Nobody. Push pull rattly screen doors & peer in vague windows. Doesn't seem to be
anybody around today. Sunday. I push a gate that won't shut. Celia says "Why isn't
anybody home?" One of those good questions. Finally try a house way back down
by fork of mainroad, a guy working outside with tools says "We're weekenders.
Somebody bought the cave beginning of summer. I don't know anything about it."
We go further back down mainroad to Williamsville Inn. Park, B & me walk around
bushes hear some voice yelling HELLO? Kids on roof fenced-in with chairs & loud
Rock&Roll Stereo that B says later remind her of some Manson scene, "the way that
girl kept talking about shotguns . . .". They say lotsa people been in this summer
anyway, we can go around back of their property & follow the river to ravine where's
the cave. We say OK thanks & I figure I can find my way in along bottom of Tom
Ball ridge. We get flashlights cameras etc & hike in across field to end of dirtroad.
First follow sorta-trail that winds up & in but seems to go too high up on mountain
too far to the north & ends up going the wrong way. We all come back down to end
of dirtroad again. Celia's up on top of big mound of sod meanwhile we're discussing
what do & says, "Are we caving?", evidently thinking that "caving" is looking for
caves in the woods. Actually this time that's right we are(!) B & I finally get it straight
that what the kids said was _not_ follow trail but follow stream. Stream at this point is
little trickle in midst high grass & bottom mud & I figure there won't be much water
in the cave. All through this hassling bustling around loud stereo floats over all:
Bonzo Dog Band, Stones, unknowns. B & I cut off ducking thru trees under vines
& shit looking to hook up with stream further in. "At least we're going in the right
direction". We find an old car beached in woods rotting interior crap falling out,

springs. "How'd they get <u>that</u> in here??" Press on, find stream meandering around, drying up. We figure this is OK & try find our way back to others thru opening into maze of highgrass meadow paths. Get all fucked up in weeds but get back & tell everybody this way. We all go back in, Celia on Susan's back, Ed with camera pack, etc. Ed tells Susan by-the-by that Bernadette is world's fastest walker in the woods. We keep following stream now dried up & branching uselessly. I make long solo looksee up ridge aways here, but figure we're still too far North on ridge. We keep going & come out in some back farmer pasture with dirt road going in vaguely right direction still. Decide to follow that. Maze of trails heading up toward ridge. Which one? Finally I recognize proper trail from times before, the one that connects directly from now-posted meadow entrance. We go up, gets steep over left lip of cave ravine. Dry as bone. Celia hop skip & jump. Get to Eldon's sinkhole up top & sit. Mosquitoes swarming around as ever tho no water in hole. Confusion as to who's going in, who carries what, what flashlights etc. Celia wants to charge right ahead in no light. You have to duck down slot tween two rocks & slip in under shelf to flat low space (tunnel) to the right. I take off jacket to feel smoother in closerock space. Somehow it appears that I go first (with light), Celia next (no light), Ed next with heavy unwieldy fluorescent tube light for movies (& additional flashlight), Susan next (no light), Bernadette decides to stay out. We scrabble in this order to end of first straight piece (20 feet or so), turn corner. I go ahead a ways, stop, turn flashlight back for Celia to see to come on. She's just the right size, can practically walk upright thru low tunnel. I've got bag containing Bolex, film, candles matches, trying contort to keep it up out of water which appears still in low (2 inch) pools. Water is so clear over marble sometimes you don't even see it till you feel it with your ass. Slide scrape & urge onward. A few more turns. Cave keeps running straight then turns a corner then straight awhile then another corner—you never can see more than about 20 feet ahead at any one point. At this point a discussion: should Celia continue? She wants to, enthused, but worried about water some, & I make quick calculation how much further (we've only come about 1/4 of the way) & figure she'll be tired out way before the end & then might stop & realize, get scared, tough (long) to get her out at any later point. So it's decided she goes back out with Susan, who takes flashlight. OK. Ed & I continue in. We come to very low (lowest in cave) flat tunnel, where you have to spread out & slide sideways keeping shoulders & legs suspending ass above water that stands in groove-channel in middle of passage. Ease

4

of cave-postures is getting complicated by attempts to keep camera-bag fluorescent-lamp high & dry. We get thru that, turn another corner, stop. Cave starts to open up more beyond this. We've made the hardest part, about 1/3 to 1/2 of the way in. Passage totally in marble now, banded in whorls of blue/black on white. A few dripstone formations, dark tan to yellowish flowstone & a few nub stalactites, kinda worn & hand-rubbed-looking, dropping from narrow alcoves above. Not too many "speleothems" (general term for dripstones) to be expected in marble cave—too hard, carbonic acid solution needs softer limestone beds to pick up & deposit out anything substantial. Tunnel pointing ahead seems to grab your head & shoot you further in. Ultimate spelunker high ecstasy cry: "It GOES!!" Stop, lay flat, totally relax, look at flat ceiling in front of your nose a minute & start to think of painting. Then I hear camera-bag sloshing, oh shit! I must've dunked it in a pool I didn't notice somewhere back. Take everything out & check it: Bolex partially wet, film boxes soaked, matches useless, shit. Oh well. Camera seems to work. My flashlight looks a bit dim, but probly only in comparison to tube light. Wish I had my carbide lamp! Brighter more diffused light than directed beam of flashlight. We wonder how much battery left in tube-light, since we spent most of last night dumbly wasting juice thinking we were charging it. Wonder if when it runs out it just goes click without dimming first. Imponderables. No good to get stuck without some kind of light in here. Ed says he feels a bit tired & claustrophobic at this juncture so we decide to turn back. Notice some 1800's dates almost "professionally" carved in walls—those guys must've spent hours working with chisels! I recall it says in here somewhere (smoked on walls with carbide flame) "BIRD LIVES!"—some Lenox School of Jazz bebopper been in here too. We slosh & slog & groan along & move out. Ed. takes some footage anyway, see if anything comes out. Tubelight doesn't seem as bright as we expected in here. See a mosquito flying around pretty far from entrance. Absolute quiet in here if we don't move. & no light, not a photon, without artificials. Get to last leg, see that dim grey-blue of daylight seeping into a cave entrance. I find an alternate exit, pop up behind rock & make face at Celia across the sink. She's happy-tired falling around the rocks narrating little tales in the woods. We're out. Pack up & go back down "regular way" thru meadow & out past No Trespass sign. Fuck you, you can't keep me out of my cave!! Amen.

Beyond the point where we turned back the cave swells out larger & drops down at each turn in the passage. At one corner you slide sideways your whole bodylength thru a crack & drop two feet into a couple inches water in bottom of first of two pothole-shaped chambers ("King's & Queen's Baths") where you can stand up & splosh around & dig the marble effects. Beyond these the ceiling starts to rise by the tens of feet thru crevices that wind up up above the last main chamber. This "World's End," so dubbed, is first seen as a big higher-than-wide hole giving on a very black nothing. You drop down into this over a lip 7-foot drop onto gravelly bottom flat floor of end room. Roof about 50 feet above, narrowing to cracks. Water flows out thru tiny passage at one end we tried to "force" once but just got stuck after a few feet, could see it goes nowhere human, had to back out. Nothing to do here but look, rest a bit, scramble around, & push up & out & all the way back through the only passage the way you came down.

Eldon's Cave was discovered by Eldon French in 1875, a boy of fourteen, watching where cattle drank from pool at foot of ravine, followed it up & went in with tallow candle in a tin can (the usual cave-discovery story). Cave is 450 feet in total length. Year-round temp in low 50's. As most caves. Water temp can be low as 49 degrees at times. Cave formed in a marble "lens" (small twisted body of rock) squeezed amongst predominant metamorphics of Taconic Range. Marble is what happens to softer limestone strata when they get fired up & heaved & twisted during further mountain-building (orogenic) movements. Geologists say the range was formed from rocks originally laid down east of Berkshires & pushed up & over them down to the west. Thus no hope for extensive layerage of lime strata remaining intact to indicate plenty & big caves.

MODULAR?

I've got my sneakers on. Alphabet.
The Cave.

Dictionary definitions. Do these single letters belong on the page,
only words belong on the page, an equivalent of bricks.
Hello.
What are you invited to do with this my page.
E.g., I still havent finished studying Wittgenstein so I dont know what
to do next, that is, what would have been where this is
I dont know what the idea i dont know the idea that comes next,
not which idea:

Blouses without shirts, tied
I mean blouses for breasts & breasts in blouses, some pulled tight so
you could see the shapes of the bodies of thought of the women who own them,
who invest them & plan to wear them & wore them, see-through
& tied in back
Black
Yes breasts You dont write around the words you dont really write around
them, Period.
I'll remember that one—its not a dream its a whole body of work I reviewed
(with you) theres no way to forget it.
Sake.
Record sake.

Different kings of type. Kings I mean kinds, Dreams. Sex without stimulation.
Sex w.o. stim.
A white chicken is visual.
Hashish is a mountain.

Directions for putting words together—accurate information combining process
with end. wds. w. end. result an absence of product maybe completely

work in one place—duplication multiplication, only information is transportable,
but not precious or, a work that cannot be moved, as, as,
precise information from say many fields
one two three environment defines what is sculptural: wds. (the cave) were
all over the paper, it is not necessary to say what they were it is not a
game to figure out which they were, they were composed of letters from a to z,
they all apex they all appear in _____'s Dictionary, but not in the order
in which they appear on my (the opposing) page, for ex,, now i'm going to tell
you exactly what happened, but wait a minute, e.g., instead of putting one page
in each book putting two or more identical ones in each each alike? Going a few
steps further, like a shooting schedule . . . for the cave?

INTRO. really afraid of losing something is it far away or in with the trees
warm bread. synergy. example, example of blood continuously flowing but the
sun with your ass, something in a dream about paying for something everything
here, reminds me of change of being transferred of being brought out of being
illumined, we have lotsa money, of being taught & trained of being inching
towards something the grass & leaves are almost invisible the windows of the
house wont open they are closed everything about here reminds me of some part
of myself of terrible pain & ache for the pleasure of denial everything about
here reminds me of some fault in interest or hobbies about here swells of being.
someone else how easy its been

bees & sun a wreckage storms never rage when you need them, I see the point of no
raging anger being at the sharp of once as victim & one as cloth. Energy destroys
it, energy warmth as pain & drift I inch I give I ignore the new words I hear & fight
them. they arent you, I'm using you, you pass by you pass through here you've got
my name wrong my name is like ice the winter weather the bear in hibernation these
words can now can finally be thrown away Clark eats away at the pronoun I & I eat
Susan's warm bread & strong sense invisible did enter them here to discard them to
allow you to discard them in any season in every season like protection from bees

Something is reliable nothing much lives in caves everything generates fear
& destroys it anything destroys it pestilence was once a thing that was opened
doubt & hesitation like I deny you is crusty, planned that way & whole windows

fenestration balustrade empty mountain underground deep even here trip of time untime you get away with nothing anything & so on it eats up time time is dissatisfied with the way things are, what things are what is a question, someone will explain it, its unconvinceable—conceivable it cannot be convinced I have to use it

It corrects stands up & weight the weight is on your back at the small dont care stain the rock with reddest blood what a thing once more to get away with a presence what one to be denied as if it once more was is or something isnt sure of, negative space, an empty drone or drome. I insist on continuing continuing country whatever writes itself in the air. I am sure you are there in the house. I am sure you are there in the cave & will come out it is impossible to get away from anyone it is impossible to use leaves as you show them it is impossible to locate space & anyway surround it even almost completely a slow progress of revelation I decide to ask the rearranging question is it why wait you are so patient you are so dream once or twice a year & I am

I guess theres hardly any way to finish it its time to wake Ed us & go to our cave deaths for sure arent we manufactures of swim blood are storing are in our bodies in our ear & sweeter ear known is as known for sure, to obfuscate more besides identities shown, almost completely exhibited, almost completely shore & wait for more, i'll tell you i'll never take one again to show alot of iron feldspar & tin flow like rivers from the mouth of the cave that will eat you, find a spot & tense & tenser words between them why are they eating why are they waiting so long whats the difference between what they say & what they drew in pictures at night that we couldnt see

they're ready to describe them they leave some things out walking down the woods is what you notice some things get pointed out, eyes tuned to dream all over the dream space extends forever theres no end to it, eye space tuned to dream, space, eyes tuned to woods, all eye space accommodates movement directs toward it movement is an endless surround an endless depict, the trouble with style, come out come out wherever you are its time to go to the cave there are scared white-haired slaves hiding there & my picture of you is a drift one that bleeds, accomplished revisions, drew crowds & was changed ever since like once you wince I leave that out, I wish I could break through the code & curtains around it & notify me as soon as you wake ate, sentries enter & order the floor, this one is quaking this one is bent summer measure is over if you drift north to see the foliage its fine crispy & ready to change. Change means fall off. You get in. You are moved from the surface, everyone's the same—sound of wind, pincers moving a murdered prospect design engineer no fear no image so must be fear I tried to stay here longer but the rock I am sitting on grew & burst in red flames underneath me made a kind of sac or hole in its own matter a new texture for gray, feldspar & granite, a pure slate rock. Of course that was me. 2 mountain ranges in space—something is in the cold something is in the clouds, something is not in the hose, you are the clouds

You are not the hose, patent leather expensive patents—everyones designs are bleeding fear & no one can mention it for fear of the trailers hooked up, long lines, back of the single energy word. What a supposition, once more then so, you can throw that one away for good I'll eat it again for you—Fear sure another, its simple & has designed a simple space, you dont agree you more a part of, you what I own sink into the same, we share it that is, so move around & expect a rest sooner or later & sing the best songs, I am hurry I am hurrying, we have to go to the cave, again I say, the best leaves wont work anymore, everyone's busy, everyone has plans, & since they can move & since they can move independent & since men & women can they dont move me directly they dont sympathize with me

The words—I'll use them all I'll set them I'll get away with it deep earth the courage it takes to dry like a tent in the sun. So many absences for covers—a scene to speak an unrehearsed cone echoes out, of itself, a spring, a spewing, a spitting, stopped on a dime, what was the experience you tell what started it, what did you bring with you, I'm outside, what did you need that you didnt bring repressed emotions are all over the messy tables, so what? skunks smells up to a certain level up to a certain pitch are fine. the biblical finals are driving there on their way home—all able to stop to eat, why wouldnt we? who says better? who the crutch fuck says even divine?

Whats the elegance of any crush whats the space of 4 people moving depending somehow on you & new ones to enervate on your way home—only the real strong &

obvious are shared, like blind chickens bared for frying or something but the real small defining ones small so are wasted, wasted out to sea, wasted one by one wasted out one by one one at a time by one or another one a different one by the way what work do you do so the reason I mention work is there's some things I learned from you & i dont stop to listen normal I steal & sink ships & yours aspect just seems to be one of them oceans no grudges against what they receive in a storm so such is not of their doing hard away from their design they have none endless they fill the frame

With much better than plan only spots of sun & parent bugs strong ones of all colors, if you're so screech scared then how can waiting you lie in the grass, something must hold it together sensible that is to touch out like everything & start it all up forever that is again & again, something must by peace of nature come out of parent nowhere & part with it to make peace & leave a piece behind as part of it addressing you, continuing on. Ice is cold the same substance is heat I saw you once before as once is twice & nearly ready they had said it would be lost they had said it would be closed. So space subsumed a minute or so of itself then someone else could enter in its obvious the drift is not in schools

Pools of energy while you wait for worth. 5 & dime. A criminal's crime. an abscess or sore. Insects that bore. Potato. Loaves. The incense of corn. The pestilence the rape. The hairy ape. An artless A core A trip to the middle go back 4 more stores, a rock a stone spreading pebbles the country is harder than leaves that it used to be the country is resistant to flame disillusion it, you spoke in the dark last night I talk in the invisible cant be heard, lined up, so what, what a shelf what a remote line up the hill lets cut in lets drop a line lets let fall a stone pebble down canyon grand mile thousand speak exhaust fumes the sensible expected & so so far we have had to have rules period.

But overnight everything changes & washes at away where we stay & study for a while. Some space.
                    Gets hot. How do we get started you is waiting 2 get going let's see go.
                    Residue can be chewed as lawns mowed for a residence which even can be moved in mass by people who do that.

11

I do. That is defined.

You dont
pay. All the tricks of the monsters of the past came to help him move the house.
I mean all the knowledge of the tricksters of the future emerged from their
temporary dip to remove it, it'd been moved before. I mean all the ink pens of
the distance stanchioned the structure of the building to be moved. I mean all
the mobsters of the present devoted action to rough up the foundation. I mean
all the trees that cant be seen are uprooted. I mean all the nests above
mountains overturned. I mean all the insignificant revolutions of the earth on
its axis is stopped come now.

Only time, to. Gotta go. simple measures.
I'm being watched, bled.

& the boat went down

2 the island. Even though they watched us,
they had to let us get out & run around

the blue steps,

timing us.

12

KARSTARTS

It's a sunday afternoon I've got my sneakers on. The car in pieces in a room. We pack up in the cave. A cave in pieces, an alphabet of several colors registers. Ed Bernadette Susan Celia & CC. Modular marble closed over them and left. The cave crosses the turnpike. A closed drive down through definitions. Turn right in the dictionary a little ways. A dirt road of several colors closed over them. The ways right and left. Dictionary definitions turn over them. A code of marble registers: E.B.S.C.CC. Do these single letters belong on the page. They only belong on the page, an equivalent of the gaps in the meadow stonewall I remember.

The bricks, being single, of several colors, turn up right, left. The lots, of other times here. The memory of a meadow's photograph hello. This time there, lots of other times here. Big new white sign says Cave Gap, Public Equivalent, Invited Hello. A photograph's silent as a definition's closed. Last there last year there. What are you invited to do. Big new white page closed to public registers. Just a little to do with this my page. Flapsign on a tree: e.g.

There was there just a little word last year, an equivalent gap. You are invited to point in with the arrow to a field with this page. Hello. Cave. What to do. Words trespassing only on the page. Consternation pissed-off studying Wittgenstein, hmmm an equivalent of bricks.

Drive down to the end of the dirtroad, turn around, start studying the main highway in person once. The cave in person once a cavern turns up. Right. Hello. I still haven't finished so I don't know. That is what to do. What to do next. Bricks are the only equivalent that belong in this meadow. Equivalent of words in a meadow on the page. Kate can skate 'cause Kate can't skate. Otha Street on another page.

What would have been, where this is what you are invited to. Wittgenstein knocking on doors and finds the new owner. Hello organized in the main. Within my page that is opposite. I don't know what the idea I don't know is opposite. Pointing to the cave that would have been where this is. The main idea within a cavern that comes next. What to do, not which idea. The idea of the cave is left within besides.

The cave without a ceiling, blouses without shirts tied by Julie Harris. An internally organized ceiling closed to the public. Nobody, push-pull, takes the blouses for the breasts. Some pulled tight so pissed off. I know the idea that comes next: blouses for breasts (Wittgenstein). Julie Harris without shirts breasts tied tight with shirts without shapes no thought of the women who own them. Probably landgrubbers who don't even live around here. Breasts without definition as bodies of thought. Alphabet blouses. The thought of ceilings and their word equivalents. Nobody home.

Some blouses mean the breasts invested in them. Peer in vague windows a ceiling goes on in. Try next house. The caverns in the bodies of thought of the women who define them (Julie Harris). The shape of Julie Harris' breasts studying Wittgenstein. The thoughts of women a little ways in caves. See-thru photographs of marble ceilings. A page, pushpull, nobody finishes, tied in back. Around in back would have been where this is. The which idea.

All sunday to mean the shape. Julie Harris in black visible in back. Doesn't seem to be anybody around sunday. Yes nobody. I invest them in back, an idea of what comes next. Finally try a house, an equivalent of bricks. Wittgenstein plans to wear them and wore them. I push a gate that won't shut. Celia says "Yes". One of those good questions if one could see it so. Yes words you don't write around the breasts you don't really write around them. Finally try a house by fork. Blouses in the shapes of houses. Ceilings incidentally organized within a jungle. The jumble of words on a very long one's arm. The period at the end of one of those good questions. A Julie Harris that won't shut.

You don't write the words that shut up. A guy working in see-thru black by fork. With tools say period. I'll remember that one isn't anybody at home. As long as one's blasting it's not a dream. It's a whole guy outside the body with tools he says. I reviewed a whole body of work with you. We're weekenders. It's one of those good questions there's no way to forget. The words for what would have been where you don't really write. A question of black gates pulled tight. Celia says "a dream isn't something I forgot about".

The thought of the what idea not the which idea. A ceiling goes on in around the words so. An equivalent of marble to do with this page. I don't know somebody equivalent to the cave. Forget it. I'll remember that. I don't know anything about it. We go back down to the beginning of summer. For the sake of parking and another and more sake. We record the sake for the sake of being now in one place. Record for the sake of now. Somebody says I remember the cave beginning at the beginning of summer. Different kings hear voices. Certain that the cave is now in one place except in one's idea of it. I don't know how that idea comes next. I push a gate that won't shut. B & I walk around bushes to hear some voices. Different kinds of parking. Definitions of different bushes. The kind that is found in moments. We know nothing for the record. I mean kinds at the moment. A whole body yelling hello. Dreams fenced-in with chairs and loud sex stems. Rock&Roll says B later. A white chicken is visual enough to remind her of some Manson scene. Some later kind of equivalent. Chairs later remind me of fences. Roofs of bricks. Marbles of ceilings pulled tight so you could see them in back. Black kids in stereo. The idea of sake while studying Wittgenstein (I didn't finish it).

Houses fenced-in with chickens. The kinds of dreams that are sexual enough to be without visual record. The women who own them. The breasts whose single letters belong in dictionary definitions. We go further back the way that girl kept talking about. A mountain of white chicken in one place in one moment. Except this is one which is found in moments. Recording shotguns and different types of type. The stimulation to forget it. That which was found in one place moments ago. A mountain certainly very long as it is now. Anything as it won't shut. Julie Harris doesn't really write that I'll remember.

You don't write to forget it's not a dream. Sex without kings without type without blouses being visual. Some white hashish is visible. Lotsa people been in from the mountains this summer anyway. They stay fenced-in in back talking

15

about Manson. We can go around in back of their property. The loud period which is found in moments. We find the river I can't forget in moments. Where's the cave which is certainly very long and incidentally organized in one place. We say it's OK without the whole body of the mountain. A jumble of different kings. I figure I can find my way in without directions for putting words together. They say the party that goes into it has accurate information, certainly reputed combining photographic process with the cave's end. We say OK thanks, we can go around back of where words end.

The marble resultant an absence of product. The cave may completely work in one place except in the one that it is now. The end means what is not found in moments. The dream of accurate information along the bottom of Tom Ball Page. Chairs without end. We make our way combining its process with an absence of product. We get flashlights and cameras which may completely work in one place. A ceiling goes on and on. Putting the flashlights together end-to-end may reach in across the field to dirtroad's end. Result: a duplication of the absence of multiplication. The directions for a multiplication of words may not work in one place in the usual amounts in many fields. Diurnal white dreams are a whole body of the visual. Duplication of the fences chairs of the gate that wouldn't shut in a moment. Only our information is portable as we wind in and it turns out.

A work that cannot be moved goes on in one place. We follow the first trail combining process with talk but it seems to go too high up on the mountain. Cameras and flashlights are not precious, not very precise information. We end up going the wrong way from say many fields. I don't know what the idea is that cannot be moved. I've got my sneakers on.

An absence of alphabet for putting words together. Celia says "one two three environment". Words carved in marble define what is sculptural but not transportable. They say lots of people been in this summer. The party that resisted multiplication took up short. Where's the cave. The words without end. The duplication of words from many fields. Escorted feet were all over the paper. They were not necessary to what they were. Words it is not necessary to say were

16

it. They Were It is not a game. The game was to figure out what words were the cave. I figured I could add spaces to the end of the knotted cord. Directions for putting words together end up going the wrong way. We all come back down all over the environment in many fields. It is not necessary to say where we were. The paper composed of the letters from a to z. Celia's on top of a big apex they all appear in. A whole dictionary of end spaces, but not in order. Meanwhile we're discussing a mound of sod, what to do and say. We all appear in the order in which the words appear on my page. The opposing viewpoint remains in the Environment Dictionary.

Now I'm going to tell you what we're evidently thinking. Dictionary. Are we caving? Waiting a minute but not in that order. Most telling is thinking that caving is looking for caves in the dictionary in a blouse in the woods. Actually it's this time and that's right and we are. But not in the order found in moments. B & I finally get it straight putting one page in each one's book of words for speech in many fields. What the kids said was not exactly what happened. But wait a minute, a white chicken is visible. That must be the mountain that follows no trail but a stream. Add this to the end to duplicate its actual length. Putting two or more identical ones in each adds a good big inch to our steps. Are ones in each each alike? The stream at this point is a little trickle in the midst of getting wet. Alike as the feet.

High grass multiplies bottom mud in the formation of its room. I figure on the paper going a few steps further. There won't be much water at the end of a perfect inch. I mean dreams of kinds. Nobody home but identical ones. The water won't be that large in the cave. All through this stereo is a floating schedule for the cave. Enough light water and words for the cave? Hassling around bustling through a loud intro. One with formations in its room. A schedule in our way. Really afraid of losing something. Is it far and away our flashlights? Or dog band in the trees stones in warm bread. Unknowns far away within the shooting schedule. The opposing dictionary floats over all.

B & I cut off a perfect inch from the five colors of dogs marble blood cord money. Example of the trees continuously ducking. Ducking to look up under the stream. Looking to hook up with the dictionary further in. The direction of the example of the sun hooking up with your ass. Julie Harris on Synergy. The right direction at least on lots of money. Everything in a dream about paying for something. Old car on continuous beach. A change reminding me of blood being brought out, being transferred in the woods. We find money being illumined. Streams falling out. Inches being added to the end spaces. Beings being taught and trained towards something. Breasts being tied in back. "How'd they get springs in here?" Something the grass and trees are, almost. Press on into the rotting interior, windows falling out. Marbles meandering around drying up. The houses won't open they are closed. Celia says "nobody". I press on the gate almost invisible from the windows. They close about everything here reminds me of some part of another range including surrounding the large end slots to be reached. We figure this is OK and try to find our way back to others thru opening into some part of myself. We all go back in moments to a maze of aches and pains, such that it is those that have ropes indeed. We have lotsa money, get all fucked up in weeds.

The pleasure of denial of everything about getting back to tell on everybody this way. There are five inch colors of marble to remind me of such a fault. Faults are interesting or hobbies are swell. Celia's on Susan's back. Ed swells with camera pack. We all go back in. Everything about here reminds me of everybody, including the large equivalents of how easy it's been. Someone else reminds me of the cave to be reached. Everything towards the house won't open. Ed tells Susan about swells of being. A rope left in water we'll call it. You can tell a sneaker how easy it's been worn. I mean bees in the sun and a wreckage of water dreams in the world's fastest woods. Walkers never rage when you need them. I see the point. And left the water worn.

Cloth being as sharp as once it was. Safety we'll call it. An anger-being kept following the stream. Energy destroys it, branching uselessly. Inches inside the rock we'll call it. The drift has dried up. I inch pain to give warmth and ignore the cloth I was given. I make a long solo of the new words here. They aren't you but figure we're here too. I hear the ridge inching and fight them. I'm using our last good big inch to pass by you.

We're still too far through here. Caves are warm as words and drift an inch. A looksee in the Far North. They aren't you. We keep going and come out with my name wrong. I'm using the energy of words to pass through here. Some farmer stands out behind his house in back. Wittgenstein's got the wrong name. Words keep going in and coming out a dirt maze opening into an inch. We all go back in hibernation. My name is in the right direction still. Like ice the bees pass. You've got my name. Which one of these words can be finally thrown away? The decision to follow a course of hibernation or multiplication. A flashlight can finally be thrown away. Julie Harris bears these words now. Clark eats away at the pronoun I sense invisible. A maze of weathers heading up to the head. We pass Clark recognizing them but which one? The pronoun I ate was a discard. Susan's warm bread enters them here each in its season. Finally I recognize the times. The one that connects properly to the entrance. Enter them here and discard every one as a protection from bees. The meadow one all laid out in formation we'll call it. We go up something reliable. Nothing much lives in caves. Everything generates bone. Everything left destroys the connections. The left lip was once a thing that was opened. We go up, get steep.

The hesitation I deny you is crusty and branching uselessly. Decide to follow opened doubt. Some farmer pasture with dirt road was planned that way. I recognize whole windows from stills before and sit. That is those that have ropes indeed. Celia skips anything. Dotted lines to the ends of the map. An empty balustrade of the now posted meadow. Planning the way to whole windows we put Eldon up top. Marble with what one took to get wet. A mouser practicing fenestration. An empty mountain deep underground. Confusion as to who's even here. We get around as though no water around. Anything trips up time. You get away with nothing as to who carries something. Wittgenstein was in a hole. Time for you to get away and so on. Celia is dissatisfied with the way flashlights are. The way things are what things are is a question. I deny you, empty mountain.

Set up a sinkhole and sit. He got away with a definition of multiplication. An untimed balustrade etc. Time is dissatisfied with mosquitoes swarming. You're going in with nothing. What is a question. Who's carrying what. Confusion as to what flashlights will explain it. Celia wants to charge it but I have to use it. Ropes inside the rock we'll call it. Someone will call to explain it. Actual end spaces are inconceivable. It cannot be convinced I have to use it. No light, right in, corrects it and stands up. The weight on your back is the small dot between rocks. The weight of a small donut stains the rock. Celia wants to take down the shelf. Once more the reddest blood, what a thing to get away with. What with one in no light right now. I don't care what a thing was if it once more is. What a thing is it is once more. You can't get away with nothing in an empty mountain.

Two rocks duck in and slip down. What a presence isn't sure of is negative space. A low space room an inch to our right. A negative presence is once more to be denied. No water in the hole. I insist on continuing what an empty drone isn't sure of. With flashlights etc. Negative weight is flat and low. Celia wants to slip in under a duck. Whatever writes itself in the air continues in the house. I take off jacket to feel smoother. I take off the air itself to feel right. I am sure you are there in the house. I am sure the cave will come out. I surround a duck between two rocks. Whatever writes itself in the cave will come out as is. It is impossible to get away from anyone if you are there. Somehow it appears smoother at first in the light. It is impossible to use anyone as you appear to them. Somehow it appears that I go first. I am sure that you are light in the house. It is impossible to locate Julie Harris in space. It is impossible to leave as you show up. Somehow I use leaves in no light. The continuing country writes itself in the air.

What one would deny an empty drone or drome. I insist on continuing to get away from anyone between two rocks. The duck will come out. It would appear to Celia. I am sure that there is air in the cave. Anyway enough to surround it. It is almost impossible to use leaves to locate space. Or even to locate leaves in space. No light. Ed decides to ask the rearranging question through movies. An unwieldy fluorescent light tube for the breasts. Wittgenstein writes in the air it is impossible to use. A slow process of disappearing from everyone. An additional flashlight. Added to the end spaces it bounds to its actual length. I decide to ask why wait to rearrange scrabble. Susan next lights on the ceiling. A question goes on in so. You are so patient to the end of the first order. You dream once or twice a year. And I am next. I guess there's hardly any way to finish the first piece (20 feet or so). Turn corner. The pages are so patient. And I stop a ways inside the rock to wake Ed up.

Cave deaths stop and go in one place. Our cave is over for sure. Aren't we manufacturers? Turn a flashlight in on Celia. See in one ear to come on. Our bodies are storing our identities as shown. We're just the right size. Manufacturers of swim-blood tend to obfuscate the sweet corn. A bag of ears. I can walk as is known for sure forever. The Bolex turns a corner. I've got a bag containing a lot of iron feldspar.

The tin flew like a river in the air that accommodates movement. They use feldspar as an iron. I'll tell you I'll never take one again. Our film matches our candles. I'm trying to contort it to keep it up out of the Bolex. Bags are almost completely exhibited. Our identities keep it up. Water appears from the mouth. Find a spot and tense the tin flow. It'll take a lot to show the tin rivers. The cave that will eat you. More besides identities shown in our bodies on the shore. Films are tenser words. They find what they are eating between them. Low water is still tense. Rivers are tenser. Why are they eating so long. Nothing running the whole year around. What's the difference between what we say and tenser words. They drew in the pictures at night so we couldn't see them. Water is so clear over marble that the difference is multiplied. A definition of a spot's the difference. Words as tense as pictures made it that we couldn't see. I'm trying to contort to ever see it till I feel it. Rivers so long what's the difference. The night ear on the iron spot.

So many pictures at the time we couldn't see your ass. So much marble over the mouth will eat you. The Wittgenstein show will draw more and find a spot. Walking is when you notice some things get pointed out. Clear it with your ass to describe them. Leave a few more turns things out. You can never see more than you're ready to describe.

That some things left out get pointed out is what you notice. A few more turns to even see it. The cave keeps sliding. Eyes tuned to walking down. Motes in rootbeer. Straight then turns a corner then awhile then another corner. Dream space extends straight then turns a corner. Ass space turns to wood. Slide the cave down a corridor. Knox Gelatin forever there's no end to it. We'll call it the water worm. Woods accommodate movement. Water laps an endless depict. Some things get pointed out then turn ahead at any one point. 20 feet of shoes. Movement is endless direction. Then it turns a corner. The trouble with style is an endless surround. The trouble with style is you can feel it with your ass. Never more than at this point a discussion. Come out wherever you are. Paris pacific in concert as concept a continuous right turn. Mine.

It's time to come as you are. It's time to smell. You never see more than Celia should. She wants to worry about water some. The trouble with movement is a matter of cave time. A quick calculation of how much further white the hair should turn. We've only accomplished about a quarter of the revisions. A tire in the figure. My picture of you is a drift one that bleeds. She'll stop hiding and drift before the end. White-haired slaves drew crowds. Was Wittgenstein changed ever since you left that out. Bar sinister. Photos of feet in several color registers. Crowds scoring a tough later point. Once you wince I leave that out. The code breaks out way before the end. Wish I could tire out that way. Sneeze revisions. Plastic bark curtains. The laugh I wince to leave off. Julie Harris figures she might stop and point.

Hiding, all of whose hair turned there, bleeds. A cake is accomplished. Curtains for its hair and it. It's decided once you take flashlight. I wish I could break around it. An apple by means of code. Notified me as soon as scared OK. The last marble to such an inch. They ate as you wake. A code entered the rock and ordered we call it the floor. This one then might stop. All is decided in about 1/4 of the figure. This one is bent to summer's measure once over. Once summer is over you get in. Foliage take the flashlight. Ed and I drift north. Change means fall off. The ceiling goes on in and you are moved from the surface. Quakes are crispy. At this measure be ready to change. Get it? This one needs water to be worn around it. Awoke on the floor in the north.

A drifting flashlight to get her out. Whispers drew crowds. Susan backs out of the foliage. Everyone's the same continues on. Very low sound of wind we come to. Pincers moving above the bath. Prospect engineers design a flat tunnel. A murdered spread. Smooth cork goes up in prospect of no image. I tried to stay here longer but the rock kept spreading out and sliding sideways. Fear must be a longer image. The sound of everyone's the same engineer.

Left bird records playing to the point of chewing-gum on a floor. I am sitting on the longer lowest tunnel in the cave. Shoulders suspending a hole in its own matter. A marble cork in tunnel legs. Red marble grew to stay here longer. Rock above water that stands in a hole. The sound of flames is the same. Everyone sitting sideways in a groove. It's a matter of sitting on and on. Red rock screwing through the well. Ease of cave postures moving their own grey matter. Flame textures get complicated. We get to keep the granite and feldspar.

Camera bag underneath me no longer than the rock. An alphabet of chewing-gum. A pure slate starting ascent standing at slight knobs. A fluorescent sac high and dry. The matter of blood staying here no longer. Of course that was me. A cork texture and the knobs it cracks on. Attempts to keep the camera moving beneath me. I tried to stay fluorescent. Feldspar and granite getting complicated in a wall. The gaps in feldspace. We get thru that. Something that is rocks in space. A mountain range is something of slight cracks in the cold. A cold hose in the clouds it cracks on. I am sitting on no image and of course that was me. I tried to stay fast.

Stop another corner. Hearing the copper turn in the clouds. Something cold is not in the hose. Two mountain ranges are not something. You are the clouds above the bath. The lamp starts to open up in space. Cave starts to stop up more beyond this. Stop the hose for something in the cold. Something is not in the house. Less expensive patients turn another corner. You. get a patent on leather. Everyone designs the cave beyond a point. The hardest parts are bleeding. 1/3 to 1/2 of the trailers hooked up in Pittsfield. No one can mention it for the fear of the way in. Fast hearing made the hardest part. Long lines in back of the single-energy word. What a supposition: once more, then so.

We've made the passage totally in copper. The once more long then lines. No one mentions feldspar for fear of the marbles. The energy of words starts to open up beyond this point. The hardest part of wind stuck on the wall. Birds playing to whorls. Once more a supposition: the hardest part. A duplicate passage behind the single word. Supposition of words hooked up in long lines so their formations fall out. Blue copper in black light on white leather. You can throw that one away for good. I'll eat it once more then. So you can hear the band for good. Heavy fear of sure light. Dripstone went heavy and dropped out beneath the flowstone. A yellowish tan. A simple man you don't agree with some part of. You drop another space and don't agree. Wittgenstein's Alcove.

You own what I sink into the same. You move a part of the marble cave. We share what that is. I design a sink in a simple space. I'll eat it again for you. Not too many move around. Speleothems sing the best songs. Hand-rubbed looking. They expect the rest. General terms to be expected sooner or later. I am hurrying so that a deep breath moves around. Carbonic acid needs a softer solution. We have to go to the cave.

The light went heavy and dropped an inch. The best leaves won't work anymore. Slight bath above limestone beds. Again I say that so deep a breath cracks. Pick up the best leaves and deposit them in bands. Coppers. Everyone has plans. Since they can move they can move since. Julie Harris pointing ahead seems to grab her head and shoot you. Everyone's out of anything. Independent men and women can pick up and move substantially. A deep breath taken in an inch.

Softer beds don't move me directly. Don't move in an inch in solid feet. Don't grab your head and sympathize with me. This here, that there. The words pointing ahead seem to shoot you further in. I'll use them at all. I'll set them flat in ceilings. A drop against the brains. The courage it takes to dry deep earth. The ultimate spelunker'll get away with it. If the earth had any the marble had none. A tent in the sun. If anything it goes. Stops in the earth. So many absences for covers. A hand-rubbed cry and the shirt lay flat.

The scene to speak of an unrehearsed cone. Totally relax. A drop covers up. A look at flat ceiling completes walls and roof. An absence of covers echoes out. We lay flat and lack copper. I'll eat one again for Wittgenstein. Again I say a cone of itself. Deposit your head and cry for cover. Spring stopped on a dime. You look at the ceiling in front of your nose and tell what started it. It's time to spit. It's time to tell it what started you painting. What marble did you bring with you. Water echoes itself. The painting completed the walls sent back echoes. Did you stop to bring the dime with you. Spring itself is what started it. I'm outside to come to think of it. What did you need that you didn't bring the thermometer. Light exceeding running. Skunks sing the best songs. It's time to smell up to a certain pitch. I didn't notice someone's back.

A certain level of certain pitches is fine. Unrehearsed biblical finals. Then I hear I didn't notice to check it. Timing everything under a completed roof. So what drove there on the way home. Take everything out and pitch it in a pool. All who are able stop to eat. And why not cones? The Bolex partially stopped on a dime. Who says shit somewhere. A certain pitch could exceed the marble. Crack on a dime. Whose crutch checks the front of your nose. Skunks you brought with you. Shit on the way home. Tomorrow's gonna be partially wet.

Marble a partial pitch beyond those numbers' extent. Boxes of words seem to match well. Camera seems to work in this marble timing. Where's the elegance in Orange Crush? My flashlight seems to work somehow on you. Four people moving the space depending somehow on new ones. The depending word seems a bit dim. Thermometer numbers on your way home. The house only seems to work. Obvious multiplications are shared. A tube full of blind chickens in comparison. Probably only numbers in the light. Real small defining ones or something.

The thermometer hose in comparison to the tube light. Numbers now wasted since we spent last night. One by one at a time by one or another one a different one by the way. Wonder if when it runs out it just goes click. Small out at sea. I learned things are at one remove from you by the way. One juice at a time without dimming first. I mention work on imponderables. No good to get stuck on and in the wall. I don't stop to listen without thinking first. Chickens are bared one at a time. Reasons I mention are tied in back. I steal and sink ships without wasting juice. Breath crammed against the brains. Your aspect just seems to be another one of those. No grudges against a directed beam. What imponderables are they about to receive. I mention work and I don't stop. Wonder if we'll run out of one of them oceans. Four people moving dumbly dimming out to sea. Ones so small they open are shared. Imponderables turned hard away from their design. Flashlight receiving a storm. Cone screws have no click. Some kinds of lights are endless. Grudges have none. Oceans fill the frame.

Much wasted to plan better sunspots. A young woman writes a letter to Racine. Imponderables, strong ones of all colors. No good to get stuck with only plans in all spots. Ed says he feels a bit better to lie in the grass. Colors are only spots. Parent bugs are strong ones. How can you decide to lie at this juncture. Waiting is to touch out like everything. So we decide to wait for something which is like everything. Only the bugs are patient. Only a plan could exceed the marble timing.

If you're so scared then how can you fill the bag. Claustrophobic spots of sun. Feel then how that is. Much better screech of diffused bugs. Wish I had my kind of light in here. A notice walls the dates in here. A ceiling gets carved in the walls. Something must hold it together. Those guys must've been professionally sensible.

Hours spent starting it all up again. Hours over of dates over. A house held up. 1800 chisels by something natural. A cigarette backwards last year. I learned the crutch of those from you it says here. Hold it all together in a bag outside. Nature come out. Grass hoods screech then. I recall it says somewhere in here. Forever, that is, again and again. Something must be smoking carbide.

Some nowhere peace to part with it. Parents came out with it. Bird leaves a piece behind as part of a school. Parents have been in here too. Continuing footage as a part of it addressing you. Marbles sent water back again and again. Fenced-in ice and slosh along out. Bebopper moves his foot anyway.

Cold the same substance as heat. Mice slug Ed. I saw you once about the substance of it. Continue in and see if anything comes out. See who said it would be lost. Carbide bird twilight. Once before once is twice. They had said a mosquito would be nearly ready. I saw it as traveling light addressing you. Distance would be closed as I passed Wittgenstein. So space subsumed a minute. I say you once lost the tubelight. A minute substance pretty far around from the entrance. Nothing flying around if we don't move. A pretty mosquito.

They had said no light would be lost. Quiet behind as part of it. Someone else didn't think it quite as bright as we thought in here. Celia says "Quiet!" Space not a photon of its former self. I don't move without artificials. Once or so would be enough of itself. Jazz moves far from the drift. Turn on last leg. Once it's over it would be closed. Else someone could seep in it's obvious. I find an alternate self pop up behind a face. Celia drifts across the sink. See dim Lenox in daylight. Drift in space and make a face. Photons falling around the rocks. Artificial narrating the last straw. Minute glasses on a ledge of mud.

We're out in the woods. Pack up the last leg pretty far from entrance. Someone else addressing you out past signs. Tales that drift is not in schools. Absolute space without daylight. Fuck you, then someone else. You can't keep so much substance in heat. Entrance to flying footage. Latch on the woods. So minute a space is nearly ready for the regular drift. Wonder if my soaked back recalls bird lives. Pools of energy beyond the point of worth. Five drops against the brains. Turn your back on the cave swells out on a dime. A pint's crime. Although low the dime drops. Each moth turns in a criminal. The cave turns its back on insects that bore. Julie Harris turns a potato in the passage.

Loaves that drop down at each turn. The marble effects the hairy ape. Crack an incense your whole bodylength. Wait sideways for your whole worth. Ones so small are wasted. Turn in the word for good. Potato drops thru a crack. Insects that bore an ape. The first couple of inches go back to a corner. Artless energy while you wait for the sore. The rock a stone. Nothing but an alphabet in the dictionary.

The first of two potholes fill the frame. An artless core of water to the trip. A king's chamber where you can stand up. Go back for more stores. Return the cave to zero. Insects spreading pebbles. A couple of inches around the effects. The country is harder than the leaves it used to be. The country starts to rise beyond these resistant ceilings. Ed times four more stores. A hairy ape leaves the country. The queen takes a bath in falling pebbles. Art spreading. Spoke in the dark last night.

You used to be able to leave the country and stand up. Dark entrance of marble spokes. Beyond these tens of feet are resistant to crevices. Kinds of stone are all rock. At one corner the flame is resistant to disillusion. I talk to kings and queens thru a crack. Invisible water can't be heard. Tens of remote spokes lined up on a shelf. Remote control hill cuts loose. So what, what the line said. You spoke last night with a bore. The hill starts to rise, lets drop a line. Let's cut in a stone above the last main chamber. What a shelf lets drop gets cooled inside. Schools in wafers.

A two-foot marble Grand Canyon. A thousand potholes where you can stand the expected. Slide sideways and dig the exhaust fumes. So far we've had to have body chambers. A king rules period. I expect you to drop a line. An insect at each turn. The so and so line up. Parakeets on beelines. The tent thru the ceiling. Pineapples moving. But overnight everything starts to rise and wind up. Dub down passages against the brain. Marble washes away at the bottom. We study the world end for awhile. Some space is first seen as a big white inch. Nothing gets as cooled as a big black hole. How do we start you. Your lip drops down over a residue. Lawns mowed in review. Even the roof can be moved by people in mass. Monsters forced to chew on lawns. How do I get to the writing room? A bath mat narrowing to cracks.

Can't see, let's go. A vertical residue that is defined. I do. You drop down. You don't. I tried to pay out the floor. A higher-than-wide monster over a very black nothing. Water flows out thru all the tricks. A lone white moth outside a bag. Trickster tales get stuck at one end. The past came to help move the house nowhere human. I mean all the knowledge of maps. Wittgenstein forced to back out. The future emerged from their house. The monster'd been moved before. A residue of tiny passage to the end. Nothing to do here but emerge from the future. Push up the monster at one end to remove it. I empty all the very black pens of nothing. The structure of distance duplicates the marble. Nothing to do but push-ups around the building. I mean all the ink pens of the distance. A bit of a rest, clearly stanchioned. All the way back the monsters rough up the mobsters. You could see the future in the distance. We tried to force the foundation. No insects drop down from the floor of the end room. All knowledge had been moved before. I mean all the nests above the mountains overturned. I can't mean that many trees.

The insignificant revolution of scrabble. Marble moths building white nests. Pasts and futures of the foundation. Mountains fucking all the way back the way they came down. We stopped the mosquito's axis. Time thru the only passage in simple measures. I've been watched, time to go. The boat went down. Silverfish on the page. Push the blood up and out. But even though they watched us rest a bit they had nothing to do with it. Water flows out only a few feet from the island. Back through the passage the way you came down the blue steps. The last marble timing us. Time to let us get out and give the run around to them. The way we're being watched we tried to rest by force. The marble island one colored an inch. The only passage that is defined.

Eldon's Cave was discovered among dictionary definitions. Eldon French, I've got my sneakers on. A boy of the alphabet. Watching 14 caves at the foot of a ravine. Watching cattle drink, an equivalent of bricks, along the page. Studying Wittgenstein, followed it up and went in. Words beyond the foot. Hello. The usual story. I don't know which Eldon French this is. Would have seen through the cave where it was. The idea of a tallow candle I don't know. A tin can that comes next. A cave is a total body of thought. 450 blouses with breasts in the low 50's. Those who invest in them year-round. Water can plan to wear them. Yes breasts can be as low as 49 at times. As most caves, I mean kinds. The women formed a black lens, pulled tight. Small twisted body of thought, tied in back. A predominant period I'll remember. A whole body of metamorphics, with you. There's no way to forget it. Marble is what happens to dreams for the record. Plans for Taconics, fired in the back. Different kinds of lenses squeezed in blouses. Marble is what happens to sex without stimulation. 49 stems amongst water in a tin. A white limestone is visual. A mountain chicken is softer.

Directions for further mountain building, word orogenies. Multiplication of work in one place. Hello, Eldon. Studying the breasts of Wittgenstein. Marble is what happens to different kinds of kings. Periods squeezed end to end. Movements result in an absence of product. Geologists say hashish is formed out of high definition. Rocks from dictionaries. Geologists say the Taconics were composed of letters from a to z. Some fields get fired up. Some chickens were originally laid down. Pages were pushed up and over them. One two three environment defines what is sculptural to the West. Thus no hope for extensive dictionaries. But wait a minute, instead of putting pages in book I'll tell you exactly what happened. Fields in the order of the limestone remaining. Bricks intact. Julie Harris usually means plenty, over a whole body of work. A boy of fourteen going a few steps further. Each big cave as a shooting schedule. Extensive duplication, for the cave?

No one will say that every time I enter my room, my long-familiar surroundings, there is enacted a recognition of all that I see & have seen hundreds of times before. Marble of several colors registers the alphabet. In a suspension-solution, so,

the car starts we emerge from the cave live living & bricks breasts equivalent in a story story stories are already told, told to burst in like this: Wittgenstein is in suspension, Julie Harris like a cave gives us cover, she's a hoax. Two pictures of a rose in the dark. One is quite black; for the rose is invisible the car starts—we have a shooting schedule: it is nonsense it is an introduction to a style of numbers lost in sense. We eat memory for a name as dinner. You put me on to this. This is a curse incidentally organized within a cavern & within one so,

& dont talk of a white rose in the dark & of a red rose in the dark. Time passes. Jumble & certainly very long ones. Four rose of any color & five. Definitions turn right in the dictionary & close in on the center of the newspaper, close in on in like a range which is at almost completely surrounding the new stuff:

the new stuff is in code: E.B.S.C.CC. How do I recognize that this is red? (rot?) Because I have learned English ("Deutsch gelernt") Alphabet Bernadette. Do these sing through definitions? Solution-suspension: it is a game to figure out which they were the breasts, Wittgenstein, Julie, an ache here reminds me of some fault in interesting stars, them & I wore them. Together is opposite. Blue blue blue schedule body home. Please come home an absence is the main idea within a cavern & an absence is all finished so I dont know. Except that within one a cavern begins once, before once is twice abscences repeat & that that is a word that has only one sense. Repeat. That is, words something meadow on the pissed-off page'll give direction to an accumulation of the bodies of thought that dresses, wearing blouses, put an end to. Push-pull I know. We love to lose the train to loose the blouses open & to lose set free. Women in a little. Women in. Leaves are tied in back. It might be found that the same thing took place in my larynx & his. You are invited to point. What a wreckage corrects the weight of the cave beginning you notice some things without blouses & they (you) begin to be denied an idea of it, image of blue reddest blue & the grammar that is right Yes! that's what it's like. Cave. Marbles & Celia said "a dream opens doubt & hesitation like whole windows fenestration balustrade goes in goes on around the words so, which is found in moments which is tools, like, fork. Now its a rabbit is not. Its a whole guy outside the body its a master of equilibrium its sex stems whole bodies equilibrium of foot of cord of spaces that bound in leap toward its actual length (I didnt finish it) & its length is no property is not owned. The women who own them can sweep the floor & the cave's record will show them in a simple process (accurate information) with the cave's end: they are sweeping. The cave now may completely mean to change. The end means I am denied voices, certain that the cave is now isnt sure of an empty idea of it. Self, I saw it quite differently, I should never have recognized it! save for this once: I try to move my mouth as I eat, I aim at moving it, so,

dream space extends forever without blouses being visual & the woods of words bear hibernation of those good questions. Do you see a red circle over there? Do I? Ears the kinds of dreams where girls are brothers. Everyone's the same—the sound of wind, the dream of accurate information, long, no fear, no ceiling & flashlights together end-to-end. An absence of product completely works. Dostoevsky had kept a journal. But blouse tells more: there is a beautiful schedule in our way so,

I am in pain. None. I mean dreams of kinds. The stream at this point is nature come out of parent nowhere in the formation of its endless room. I am doing nothing. I am doing more. Both are amazing. Body of water with the bowl is storing, left the water torn & others, "L.W.'s pain" is a winding in & it turns out as wars wound down we fear sure another & you are in. But wait a minute—that must be mountain that follows no end to duplicate its actual length. something must hold it together sensible like feet in the formation of its room. There wont be much dreams of this kind of arm bread. Five colors of dogs continuously ducking. Somewhere in the dark last night you hooked up with the dictionary further in—everyone's the same—dream of accurate information, discussing a mound, we finally get it straight in the brush, blasting through then back to the field for an open vacation. The stream at this point is starting it all up again

32

forever & that is again & again forever & that is again getting wet, like feet, in the formation of endless few steps further toward the room. If I shut my eyes, whether I have not turned to stone & the stone will have the pains since it cannot be moved. Four or five colors my name is like ice the bees pass. I sense invisible pronoun gets hot. Monsters press on the gate. Structure this is OK so,

                                                            the house wont open
& neither will the hose is in a maze the red rose doesnt. Finally you've got words that can be thrown away. Finally mountains overturned get all fucked up in weeds. A ceiling goes on in so breasts are tied in back. Randy Newman read it. Nouns. Energy destroys it, I do not transfer my idea to stones. Stones throw up the pronoun I ate & it was even in season, the one that connects properly to the entrance. I am waiting. One colored an inch with five colors colors of the east west ridge & south along the stream stream Susan to eat Ed getting there. Now ice the bees pass. There is agreement in form of life. This goes beyond measuring: I am not sure now what I want to do. Everything generates the bone of my speaking, I am the person speaking: As you say the left lip was once a thing that was opened, the individual words of this language refer to what can only be known to the person speaking. You say, I recognize whole windows from stills before & sit, planned that way. I am that person, speaking. Celia skips anything. Therefore, another person cannot understand the language. Celia is immediate. Clark is private. Susan is sensations & I am that person speaking. The fifth colored an explorer who watched them & listened to their talk. He might succeed in translating their language into ours. Ed swells with camera pack. We all go back in. He might sense to predict he might hear them making resolutions & decisions he might sense pain. This body has extension, multiplication over hibernation. & another Julie Harris drifts an inch over the static temperature of the cave.

                        So we cannot see anything. & the bricks get away & so on. Disappointed. Weight is flat & low, fast & alike, going a few everyone to its actual length of the sound you occurred to me we mix in the cave. Brought out of being, our cave is over for sure. Its all we see about everything in one ear to some part of identities as shown. We're just the pleasure of denial we meet there finally standing up, swells of being containing alot of iron feldspar. You take off the air. Words the cave were air in the cave letters from a to z, able to use leaves to locate everything in space. Ed Celia Susan Clark & I cannot be conceived so,

you see the point that accomodates movement, You pass completely exhibited—our identities mouth. Can now can finally be shown in our bodies on the shore. The cave that will discard them to allow what they are eating between them to be here. Its time to wake us & go to mine. We'll call it impossible to use leaves as you show movement you slide the cave down the solutions to mathematical problems as they stand in relation to the context & ground of their formulation. Pain—light—science—its eye space accommodates movement & curtains for its hair its eavesdropping & it. Its surrounding I wish I could break around it for sure. My picture of you as you wake as soon as scared OK. The ceiling notifies me as soon as you wake ate this one needs water to be in the north. As soon as you show movement—wake up! water laps an endless depict. I could break around it. An intention is embedded in its foliage, its cave, its construction, its ceiling & meanings look too slight. An intention is embedded in between them to be here. You are moved from the surface & a state of confusion bars the way out. Music without the sound of wind, cork. Rock cold slate rock bars the way as a process of getting is getting faster & faster & longer, lingers to touch out like the hardest part, we get through that. 1/3 to 1/2 of the space of 4 people moving depending. They expect the rest. The hardest part of wind stuck a queer memory phenomenon. You can throw that one reaction & never speak, except to yourself. So space subsumed a general. So far we have had to have rules: a deep breath taken in an inch but,

surely the owner of the visual room would have to be the same kind of thing as it is: but he is not to be found in it & there is no outside. Dont shoot me further in. There are many stops left out in the earth & timing. The Visual Room seemed like a discovery, but what its discoverer really found was a new way of speaking. I'm outside the thermometer come to think of it might even be called a new sensation. Now I am having oceans fill the frame, now 4 people moving dumbly is a complete account of the imagined world, now obvious multiplications disapprove of the expressions of ordinary language, now imponderables, chalks, completed roofs all perform their office, now cracks in our heads conflict with the picture of our ordinary way of speaking. I steal does not describe the facts as they really mention work. Who is in pain? Another one of those.

Only the passage that is defined is in pain. I do not point to a person who would close distance for me, who could see me twice, whose pain was traveling light addressing you. You drift once & before once is twice & this can be given a justification (justifiction?). I never heard Julie Harris say anything. No light would be lost for the main point is: I did not say feel then how that is but I am a criminal like every moth. Now in saying this I dont name any person. I turn in the word for the first couple who offer a reward. Just as you fuck you, then someone else, as I groan with pain. Potato drops through a crack & someone else sees who is fucking who from the groaning. Its a trick. The rock a stone. Nothing but an alphabet in the dictionary. What does it mean to know who is fucking? How do we start you. Nothing to do here but emerge from the pain. It means, for example, to know which man in this room is fucking: for instance, that it is the one who is sitting over there pushing up the monster, or the one who is standing in that corner in the tiny passage to the end, or the one the structure of whose distance duplicates the end, the tall one over there with the fair hair & so on.

We tried to force the foundation. What am I getting at? The only passage that is defined. None. I defined it. Not quite. I want to draw attention to the cave. But wait a minute. The cave goes a few steps further. It grows the name of a person & the here of a place. Its physics can imagine several people standing in a ring & me among them & this is the shooting schedule or script:

One of us, sometimes this one, sometimes that, is connected to the poles of an electrical machine. We cannot see. I observe (I do not observe) the faces of the others & try to see which one of us has just been electrified. Then I say "Now I know who it is, since its myself" I could also say "I know who's getting the shocks, its me" But if I make the supposition by extensive duplication (in the cave) that I can feel the shock even when someone else is electrified, then the expression "now I know who . . ." is intensified & is is not for the cave.

ONLY PASSAGE TO DRAW ATTENTION
WITHIN A CELL OF ORDERING SHORTENING

No one will say "the cross" every time I enter my room, driving rocks, my long familiar surroundings, zen and others, as is enacted a recognition of all I saw and redrew and have seen hundreds of times before. Again, they cite, where, who have made the colors register, the gross alphabet of granites & marbles, expect the suspension of any like solution, to turn out, so. An equivalent, the car starts, as we emerge in minor uniform from basal basement, having remobilized the belts on all dolls and others. As from a cave, the live, the living, bricks, cross in continuous tell. As in a story, illustrated stories are already told. Thus, Wittgenstein is in suspense, Julie Harris models off her flanks to be redrawn, others withdraw behind being hoaxes. Two pictures of two rocks are too few rocks in the dark. In illustration of such suspense, one is quite black. The other, rose, is quite as rather invisible a car starts. Boulders of an earlier schedule pose the core of introduction to belts of number style. A name for memory is a chain overlain by cores the body rocks. Dinner was clear, cut thin, and at least took place. You put me on to this, the plane one each shall order. Incidentally then, at that, any waviness of array may be organized within any one. So don't talk between two times to three. Talk of a white rock in the dark of a red rock in the dome. Time passes on that, as does any colors. A uniform & very long wavelength to fix, as any rose of color. This serves the dictionary, to fix, any definitions. That local servant turned right to salt on the mantle. If a belt is to be used, as it is much, close in on the center of that model newspaper. Closing on in, like on a range, one shall see it as salt plain. Such thinness of mature position, an almost rigid surrounding, nearly stuffs the dome in separate piles, as shall this simplify. Don't let the glasses fool you. The new ratio of initial stuff is this code. These ratios of code. The code how. Breakup of red in waviness this is. Domical rot because I learned English? Large alphabet as physical Bernadette. That these do sing as large through. All these gabbro sung. The solution of definitions the suspension of salt. It is late as a game to figure out beneath the model. Pure rose. If you think that I don't. That miles were the setters' quartzite. Julie's breasts as is in Wittgenstein's basement. Accumulation pinhole. To fix an ache here reminds some of certain faults in Joseph Conrad. Interest in that dome proposed stars of certain rigidity. Between them and I wore them, out together. Blue blue is an opposite. A single biotite ode typical. Blue orders a much higher body of home. Please come home, an absence of bop brushes. Except that main bad idea within the whiskey. Caverns begin one order higher as domical serves. Some of us are growing very tired of the pain. Odds be. I just might have some thing to say. Hammond boards. But it wasn't too long. A radar of certain surface salts. Satisfies an absence in position, is all finished, escapes. Belt so. I don't know. One's name is Ray Fletcher. Back next year with radios and guys. Dome positions within one, begins once, before one's. Absence repeats that that is a word. One in a sense. Nailer to a masterpiece. Repeat something that serves a word a second. Sialic repeating meadow. Domes pissed off the page'll give a second direction. Accumulation of faces the thought that dresses. Put an end to the latter more likely order to wearing dresses. It's just the way the stars shine. I know Oliver. Push domes pull models. We lose the train and part as such. We love to lose the core part, loose the core absence. Open such as the blouse. Space women in a little. Women in amplitude, the array overlies leaves. Ate, spacing the leaves, tied in back. The same might be found in parallel chains doing so. Take place larynx and his, her larynx. As you are invited to point to salt anticlines. What ample scan dynamical wreckage corrects the weight of. Beginning the cave you notice some such without things. They are invited to begin you without blouse. Which lie in the basement, all those clouds disappear. Deny an idea of it. Image of reddest blue anticlinoria of the domical grammar. Blue of reddest blue and that is right. Paradox of your basement neighbor, whole windows of what it's like. The Yes Cave. Celia preferred spacing the marbles & those parasitic highs a dream opens. Doubt of hesitation like whole mantled salts. Fenestration goes on in around its nearest gulf. Frequency of the word so a paradox. Petroleum found in tools, like, forks. The spacing chosen to be found in moments. Now a rabbit. Now it's not, now a whole outside, now it's some hundred. Domes outside a guy. A whole body at the outside. Relative to the master neigh in equilibrium. Preferred the sex stems cored. Whole bodies, to have had to can, these be a prior equilibrium? There's a chance of thunderclap. Can a foot be bound to leap toward mean spaces? I didn't finish it, my steep bias. Its actual and length within a cell. Short of property length no gneiss is not owned. Long range short order women may sweep the view. The cave viewed as a dome will show them in who own them. The cave's record, and nearest neighbor, on the floor. At last a simple accurate animal of regional thickness. Information processed at cave's end. They are sweeping, isolating a cylinder by fluid walls. The cave may now completely change to prevent same, as those stick rocks the end means. I am denied the end means since voices are the other viscosities. Certain of the empty idea of it, a time antiform. Now time one isn't sure of it. Dome, a self of it I saw. I should never have recognized it in this salt scale. I try to move my mouth at a velocity designed to model it as I eat. I saw it quite differently at the knees. I am moving it thus, if less so. I've got to get a cross. Or dream three. Rauschenberg space extends hibernation beyond computation. Mantled blouses visual nailed in the woods. Words good as their questions rise. Dome treats as well as fluid sticks. Do you see a red cell ordering shortening? The kinds of dreams where ears are within red circles. Girls in phase are pelvis brothers. Everyone's the same Charles Bronson over there. Dream of the sound of a bean. Bulk of information, accurate along its long axis. No fear, no ceiling, one tick, so long. Flashlights tick to end together. An absence of salt ships produce. Complete & heavy, the dome works. Dostoevsky had kept a journal heavy on the quartz conjecture in partial literature. Then a blouse ticks more. A bean schedules the stress off Shearing. Varnish off a violin in a way, so beautiful. I am in our way of pain. Beans are coastal. None. I mean rocks ship dreams of kinds. At this point in nature the nipple came out of the parent. Stream of rolled garnets nowhere in formation. Hesitation natural of its endless room.

Nothing doing fast and deep seated. He had those days painting. I am doing more domes. Both decay and in stress estimates amazing. The body's belted spacing the rate of water a bowl is storing. The water left a period and others torn. You are in pain and it turns out wound down. You models are too large in case. But wait a minute, a period, a roll of tens here. That must be no end a mountain follows, driving the only subject actual to duplication. Something subject to hold orogenies together sensible like feet. Formation by seating of its room. There won't be much slower rocks. This kind of arm strains at the bread length scale. In each core are small bars in five colors of dog. Antiform continuously ducking a mean strain somewhere in the dark. Last night hooked up the dictionary with a mantle. Further in mean bars everyone does it the same. Than that now occur, accurate as to form, discussing Mounds Bars. We finally get the same straight however maximum rocks to get a dome rising in the brush with blasting out of the way. Then through a hinge, back to, open the field, above all both. A vacation rising to a core. One day I am going crazy and point and dome rises. The stream at this region of the hinge is starting in to dome it all up again. Since. Again that is the again that is again. Nailing meals to the model core in formation of endless like wet feet further. Salt poise toward this room. If eyes shut, Athens bulks to a deep seat of stone. And the stone will have poise to the hinge each move or strain. Since four or five my name cannot be moved. A stone with the pains. Color my name, pass the bees the ice, roll garnets, record elastics, get invisible and the pronoun hot. Press on like monster glacial amounts. So OK, this is the dome structure. The house won't open to show heat and neither will it hose down the maze. The red rose doesn't roll up the mantle. Finally the Navaho deviant words for "herring" and "creep" get to be thrown away. Deviatoric mountains. Creep pressures all fucked up the last ten bars. Weeds phrase quite as on the basis it is certain that a ceiling goes on in so there it is. Breasts it is quite certain are large get tied in back. An assemblage of kilobars Randy Newman reached over rock and read it as. Sure, small and undergoing nouns. That can, energy destroys it. The transfer to my idea as a stone to stones. Even stones to throw up the shape button of the dome. Pronoun can even to some extent. I ate it was what some gross can even in season. The one extent connects to the finite. I am waiting properly an entrance to minor bars. Sounding as colored to one strains. An inch with five colors little terrane. East along west kept plank to a negligible. Getting there Susan models some. Ed West now of the most final. Ice bees pass the dome. There is form to life that it can point is too. This goes beyond measuring I am not sure now what. There is large agreement on everything I want to do this. Mantric fabric of bone generates my speaking. I am as you say the person speaking of the garnets. The mantled study was once something that was opened to the right lip. A rolled history, the words this language refers to the individual. Vermont only can be known to dip to the person speaking. You say, chaired I. Whole windows sit still before mushrooms planned it that way. I am that person of moderate flank speed speaking. You say Celia ticks. Anything skips anything. Therefore stem another person shapes on the other hand rocks. Only steep language remains Celia cannot understand. Immediates remain. Clark's private strain rising in the fig domes. Susan's sensation of Athens flanges. & I am that minor, person speaking the fifth in agreement. An explorer, colored on the rim, who watched them. Inferred listen percent strain on hand at their talk. Success in translation, spruce tree spacing. A camera packs the language with reverse hand swells. All who go back in drag folds. A close dome he might sense to predict he might hear it. Decision resolution as pain of might. Body folds crest beyond multiplication. Another hibernation of no dome. Another most natural minor inch drifts over Julie Harris. Temperature of static flanks then take place of cave. So doll and others cannot see anything. A plane plunge dome bricks get away from. Down weight, an equal mum. Discs dissapointed. Flat & fast (stretching), low & alike (flattening). The model everyone goes a few. The actual length of a sound shortening you to me. Qualitative we mix rich. The cave brought out rose down the dome. For sure discs close out of being. Our cave rods have their axes distributed. We hum all about everything in one while not large. Fabric identities shown to one part of some ear. Identity of figs, the variety of pleasure. Denied our standing up we finally handed the pebble right out. Swells of flattening contain a lot of beings. A rod of feldspar irons you right off the air. Shear words to take to the air letters. Stretch cave from A to Z. To locate everything leave the space things used to take place. Ed Celia Susan Clark & so I cannot be conceived features. You see the point movement accommodates rocks within all parallel rocks. You pass in such complete a sub level the rod our identities mouth. That can now to have been finally shown. Can on shore, thus setters. The cave that will balk discards them domes. Allow them what they are eating to fold between them. It's time to link its time stretches to be here. Tense us to go to wake we'll call it. Impossible Baltimore depends to end. It is important that movement use leaves as you show. Put the cave down. Solution models mathematical problems posed. They stand in tense. A mantling stand from the ground. Formula may field a useful context. Light domes of science pain. Eye movement accommodates superposed mascara space. Intrastratal hair dropping curtains & wrapping it. I surround I for I sure could have seen at least one another. Picture break phase from my reasoning, my rotation picture of you. Picture the rocks that it wraps as soon as you wake. Ceiling notices as soon a balk near. Wake this one model needs water to be eaten. Ram rocks different in the north. As soon as show movement a spacing not fit for a mushroom shows. Water centrifuged laps and supposed an endless depict. I could break while around a uniform keeps it. An intention is embedded in fit enough tick to ask of its foliage, to ask of its cave its construction of spacing gneiss. A ceiling's meanings that lie in too slight a motion of arrow. Intentions of a disc embedded in between a rod. Centrifuge restricted them to be here and you are so moved. The ellipsoid surface state of a local model may bar the ways out. The sound of music as wired without a hot cork. Rock scales cold layers of slate for at least the rock bars the way bulks poise a process. Finger faster and longer fingers to touch out and part of the hardest pall lingers. We must get given through that. People moving a can does model the space a button depending. They expect the rest all based on increase. Hardest part of solutions stuck in an initial wind. A queer gives the model rock to his memory. Small core dome phenomenon you can throw that one. Reaction to that one does not see and never speak. That is that notice except nearly to yourself. So thick a general subsumed the dome. Rock bulks large so thick so far. The same stems to have rules. A deep value differs, taken in to the same inch. But breath differs, its scale takes in less. The owner of the surely spacing room would have to be visual. Summary same kind thing is it? But he is not found to be in it bulks when fit to. The dome that there is no outside. Don't shoot me in the rocks. There are many models stop further in. Apples from out in this earth, their growth from timing is small. The visual room seemed a visual dome, like discovery, it's what might it think of it. Apply for a new rate way of model speaking. Discoverer models rising. The thermometer outside come to as crude a new figure as now I'm having. The rim of called-for sensation. Now am having oceans fill with this sort of salt, a cliff in the window frame. Sharp people move to account for a dumbly complete imagined world. Multiplied expressions enclose ordinary language. Imponderable roofs precipitate chalks. Office cracks, both perfectly preserved and performed, older than our heads conflict. Ordinary domes in the way of speaking pictures. I steal across the facts cutting the descriptions that support really mentioned work. Who is another personal one of those. Doming up only the passages defined in pain. I do not point to the person in drag who would close in on my distance upside down. A traveling person whose light was addressing you in reverse. You could drift once and see salt twice a reversal. Internal joining this can be given one justification. I never heard Julie Harris rotating her glass. Say anything. No light would be lost from the salt starting for the main point this is. I did not say then feel. But how that is I am. A criminal like every moth rolled into a garnet. In saying this now I just name any person that starts this dome to rise. I turn in the first model words coupled with ideas as to their errors. A potato emerged, else a crack for someone else sees through its trick rock a stone. Adopted, just as you offer you, then someone else a long garnet. From nothing an alphabet in the dictionary. How do we start your numerical key. Nothing to do with it here but emerge from its domes, its examples for instance it means.

A PASSAGE TO DRAW ATTENTION OR AN INTERMISSION

The time is the present, of moves on. The silence, after a time is torn him and squashes him into the mud. Until the supply is gone. Apart by a congress of loons: ten loons, he gets up cursing me. The fault is your canoe looks Indian but you race in circles on the surface of the mine. I did not tell him where not to not do it. Water, screaming, splashing, squealing, step. Did you make them from a kit? Like dogs, taxiing in long half-flying, I stay closer to him, the better to real birch bark, is that? Runs for a full ten minutes they keep guiding him. He lifts the canoe, moves on. Where do you buy them? You move it up—a ritual insanity, a rampant short distance, then he puts the cave where it looks fake to be fake so I figured they had to be the real dance of madness, a convincing half-down. His Indian carrying board is figured to be the real demonstration that every one of them is hurting his head. Give me your jacket-thing, crazy as a loon. I give him my jacket, I've always thought it was painted on. The long carry has about every string, get me some string. From my pocket on, an obstacle a carry can have, short of Germans, I give him some cord. Terse, angry, on. Shepherds trained to kill. It has. He fashions a pad for his head & at this, those are old caves, arent they? Quagmires, slicks of rock, small hills point, Henri seems frightened and all patched up like that. Down trees, low branches, and, first, shaken with doubt. They dont make them like that angrily, distance. Three miles, even on flat rock, for its part, seems to be, if anymore, ground, is a long way. In sheer ooze anything, stronger, much of the strain. Congratulations, that's the best and muck, this portage is as he has left his face. His vitality, imitation of an ever-seen. Wretched as the Mud Pond, and is merely a specially differentiated part of it, his endurance seeming to rise a little canoe, so neat and carry. Warren departs first, bit with each part of Henri strong, drew a favorable criticism from & with a large pack and the tent, it is no longer customary to castrate people for indulging their sexual lusts, that comes unstuck. All the wiseacres among the tavern cross, return, and cross Warren passes. Going the loungers along the road he wrote. Again, nine miles. Moving other way. It is Warren, really Thoreau as he approached the woods. Alone, he escapes the compass, we know what the affective reactions to separation are. Lying, who is defeating the poor. Henri seems disappointed at the end of tension. Mike follows soon on the basis of losing the mother's breast at weaning, outwalking, outcarrying ends if no one is there. He is not after. Henri tells me not to go, employing all his intellectual faculties to that ending everyone else. He tells us techniques are disappointed now. Six men in plastic. This does not imply anxiety on my own but to stay back we are more than halfway. Canoes arrive to begin the carry. With Rick and guide and help the various situations of danger arrive one after the other, the news is surprising and, remaining at the same time connected in their origin, are they real, one of them asks. Stay close to Rick. Tonic. I look to him. My turn, do you mind if we look them in the guise of a syphilidophobia. Stay with Rick . . . Help Rick. After we know that it is no longer customary, now? He has no thought of over. He keeps saying as the three of these objections seem unimpeachable and must be given due weight, I think it is probable that giving up his canoe can be likened to an attempt at flight. Intentionally internalized, you made them? We, us go up the trail. The emblems, after another half mile of really. That Rick may collapse, and this narrating the trail, I have become both they, in turn and a second opinion, formed to avoid anxiety. To have something to tell is not lost on Rick, who is tight in the restless & guilty. I tell Henri I feel us. In Ciss Stream, which lies between the nature of women, the throat seems all the more pinned down, leading him through the long portage & Caucomgomoc, determined to carry the canoe the whole woods, slowly, while Warren is doing the initial stuff. Lake they saw thirty minutes ago, a distance alone. Henri's canoe weighs so much of the work. No one will say "cow moose" every time I enter my room. Warren arrives with the pounds, Rick's seventy. It's not the "Well, I'm carrying my share," or an obsessional neurotic prevented from washing his hands but the packs—we load and go. We wait but the bulk brings Henri's answers emphatically. Apparently it's a late game to figure out. Ciss Stream, from the portage to the cave, pure rose of the mental apparatus, light branches of balsam springily entering, he wants to believe it. Any lake does not drop one inch and is a sexual impulse of liberty, pushing the hulls, staggering the walker in ways ultimately attributable to the influence of the external world. He adds, "You have no blouse on". Warren is back. Deadwater with meanders so curving beneath. With the slightest stumble, the packer likes what he is doing. We lose the train, which is a reaction to an earlier danger, and if he recognizes the danger-situation before it has actually overtaken him & signals its approach by outbreaks of anxiety that they almost form oxbows, I dont know. Near canoes lurch forward, straining the hesitation natural to this endless room. Not far from the portage end, two silence. The third, now a whole outside, cannot protect itself from internal instinctual dangers, as no fear, no ceiling,

43

one tick, so long. We steal around its unending muscles of the legs, neck, and back. Hours after the start Henri calls for a bending through the sedge. Every existence of the second, phylogenetic factor, is based only on inference: "Help Rick!" Halt at a stream for a drink. Since four or five of my name cannot be moved, I am about. Reintroducing the old thing of defense is right. The breeze is toward Henri. Further investigations show no inclination to move to go back to help Warren, but that there is an intimate connection between special forms of defense & particular illnesses, as for instance, the possible discovery of yet another important relationship, but, Henri us. The bends conceal us. And the so. I swear it.

PASSAGE OR ABRUPTNESS

The bends conceal a pinecone, therefore a wind drawn free rather than a sequence of clothes. The breeze is toward the Modulor, a white-nights connection, the inclination of the outline of my name cannot be moved, comfortable enough to be intimate toward an essay, a hot cola in a white sky. Wittgenstein tossed a rug over his jockstrap, no ceiling on the breeze toward the muscles. Dangers tempered by defense, the finest point of Victor Hugo. I am about to open the chocolate of Charles Fourier among newspapers, hair in full spin at a stream before a mirror. A sketch of the water around its granular inclinations, hours after the moon, flat as a boy's. The silence lasts like fire, dowel bells from the portage end. The cave pinned to the white wall ticks around him, tall blue dodecahedron of Mondrian on his worktable, shows no move to intimate back to help me. Blue moon of John Russell, cowled in a dead tree, furthers existence so ring a bell. Turbulence coherent in coils to this endless room, for Wittgenstein the officiousness of a codpiece became language, the cubists wrote. He steals around every existence on inference. It was around the bend of 1914, a diving board defined by emerald boundaries: My retina, his retina. His windmill, my windmill. The Germans call a second halt, of real light, ruled into a grid. And no fear of the muscles as pictures become language. Lascaux forms oxbows from the portage end, brown chairs off that side of the house. He drinks for surface tension, the shadow on sulphur scree, particular necks of cinnamon and burgundy. The Baltic sun signals and approaches by outbreaks of sacks in canoes, squatting like foreskins in endless room. Halt at the sit-ups, ticks standing up in American tennis shoes. The aesthetic comes from the instinctual dangers of particular illnesses. The Greek measures the bike as a naked machine. And Ovid bends over Darwin, protractors with a history rather than a nature. Picasso was born dead, no fear had actually overtaken him. He leaned over the blue triangle of his notebook, writing: Man into octopus, no inclination to help existence, a plumb bob. And Henri Bergson sings a soft warm air, rich in Tang. Leibniz went upstairs to see Boyle, a room loud with Spinoza. Henri calls this cave The Paws of the Sphinx, well run and stolen from the stream for a drink. In silence time the bow, its bends conceal us.

       A yellow boat, brown under light branches, its horns of shell pearl spinning honey. No one will call the liquid silence, a vagina of zippered poplin. We load bread into the deadwater machines. Launch on lawns any lake will not drop. The sexual impulse is a liberty of cattle owners, their blades cutting iambs for the table. No blouse on in Van Gogh's spare room. A cubist painting is a marriage of canoe weights with a closed Byzantium. Insects are the enemies in turn of space. The slightest stumble in a garage papered with brown notebook pages. He arose in white cotton briefs, buttered armpits deep in flowered handlebars, to influence the external world. Today any lake packer laughs at the stink of the swinimingpool and, losing the train, likes what he is doing. Cato boiled turnips and water, pushing back the selenite hulls, an obsessional neurotic. Laforgue is back, but speech is over before it begins. Apparently it's a game all implied in the very first chord. He wants to believe that the sentence is all there in the opening syllable, light in the eye, balsam in the mental apparatus. No one will say "magnet bore" every time I enter the Lydian mode. Any lake does not drop, mirrored atoms in the depths of iron. So much of the work to an animal is food. Balzac says a man of genius will weigh his particles, across which the sky draws a white line. Vermeer pinned down zero when prevented from washing his hands. I have a place in the country, where light branches from Balthus, Delvaux, & Sassetta. The professorial tone is a sexual impulse, a narration drawn parallel with the course of a blouse. Mine are Danish. Loud pops, her hands. A tulip at a distance alone. Civilization is rooms, and the time to enter mine. An essay by Rousseau on the nipples of Gide. Deep in our dim and halting nebula, I have to avoid anxiety. In a beige raincoat I spin from my boredom, looming the initial load of a neurotic, a Greek sounds like a bird. A moon is not the well, all angle and olive in the gymnasium. There are owls here, bees, a snake in a lake. The silence is of caves. The masked silence of drawings is internalized. River rocks replaced the capitol. Colette pinned "There is but one animal" down on the page. And Poussin arrives with his pounds. Shakespeare walked each inch in ways ultimately attributable to the external world. Thought is archaic, a Mahler seeded with copper, And, so curving beneath, he wants to believe all things are signs.

The United States being an opinion of coffee, or acne in a cabin, we load in the sun and go to the moon in low voice. Taking out a pair of blue jeans I enter my room, mouth cupped to the initial neurosis. We do not eat the horse, said Pythagoras, because it is a table. A brain is a river upside down. They saw the lake in terms of writing on warm pebbles. Do not drop the Brancusi in the Europe of Picasso, the nature of women, determined to carry, in the poise of ovals. Picasso paints in Latin, Braque in Greek. Cocteau writes with spoon and fork. Apollinaire narrating this trail, our weight asleep is no longer customary. Drums are not lost on Rick, who is tight like glass, a grainy golden quartz light in his eyes. The throat seems all the more fluid as smoke, parting hair from hair in sequence. Unseemly! an angel said, as a cow moose entered my room. Henri's canoe has no thickness, in a film covering form. I have something to tell the physicist: Mozart missing the train with a trombone in his hands. The pale Egyptian insisted on distance alone. The throat seems all the more pinned down at Lascaux, breasts drawn with mammoth fat, light branches of balsam in the city of cats, Wittgenstein overlaying a Renaissance starmap and calling the sky the cave. A collapsed canoe, on which was written "Is this the Country of Soren Kierkegaard?" The Last Words of Copernicus in F Major, for accordion drum moose & guitar. A mental weather cadence which lies between the nature of women and Mondrian as a boy tying his shoe. A snail caught on a fluted column is like our canoe of a whole woods. The red dots in the dust are atoms, which do not shine on a man in flight. So does the Wittgensteinian cello of Mondrian hang in my room, the water clock of Gluck, and the soccer shirt of John Hollander. The emblems may collapse, but the bicycle, hung by its geometry, is not lost on the bottom of the sea. The film dividing the mind from the world is not lost on Rick, a glass jar of acorns on his oakum desk, photograph of the light inside water, a sweater over her head. The Seven Points of John McPhee on a blue cobalt shelf, a red ball is every color but red. A cave has no thought of cover. I look restless & guilty filled up with light, as shady as wood, tripped over the stream in balsam shorts, a triangular thinking the opposite of Rodin. Green is a tempo of light, a canoe we load to the throat with no blouse on. Sexual liberty is sometimes a ghost of the capacity of the observer to receive. Only our clothing joins together the disparate distances of flight. We see Cocteau in the Vermont hills on a Schwinn bike with phreatic eyes.

Stay close to the creek, like stalks of celery, engines with condensers in the pepper trees of Erewhon. He has no thought of saying the weight. Cities crashing into each other with great ferocity, anxiously internalized and you made them? It is a true state of terror that made the water budge. His canoe can adjust his space sense, his notebook page a flexible bright blade. His eyes looked at every face, the buttons on a vest, only the more pinned down. I have to avoid the anxiety, the pig on the tummy, the hippie branches of the Great Theory. And the stream pounds away, a diagram of lunar phases. Declare the pennies on your eyes, the roots that gave us Stan Kenton. I am determined to carry the bronze cats to the well, as professors attend to a tree near a college. Henri is an attention payer, he keeps saying that a canoe must be given the abandonment of skill. The automobile has become a cockroach and is eating the cities. A half mile of oil, as Rilke said, waxed blue linen birds in unison. To have something to tell is not lost on Agassiz. The more pinned down the closer he stays to the objections, the country of photographs in the grain of things. The giving up of his canoe can be likened to the effect of baths on the simplest brain. You knew Wittgenstein at Cambridge, didn't you? Rick said. He tied one shoelace but not the other at the bicycle races. He takes off the panties, and keeps saying You made them? In a circus, a veritable Herakleitos, he took up painting, the canoe in colors of loam and tied with string. People like eggs on sundays to avoid anxiety. The news is typographic in origin. The moon rose like cats in a chair. Sir William Herschel has whistled the planets in from the lake. Do you mind if we lock them in Ohio? Extremes can claim the greatest of poets and the worst of prose writers. A trapezius of citron from Ezra Pound in the jade stress. And Delvaux tells me not to go, missing the train and tight in the blouse. The liquid sphere of Poincare in plastic, accelerating the spin of Braque in a canoe of green. Matter is still no longer than light. And the tenor grips are opened wide over the wheat. Tangerines, sulphur, and chestnuts: the remaining dangers.

        Who are these water striders? Pinned down like a field of initial tulips to see. They occupy the same world we load. Everyone else fights reality, said Rousseau. Suffering his ghost an ugly cut, intellectual faculties to the same coda everyone else jigs to. Purple in daylight, moonlight, lamplight, if we observe them from the mother's breast. And from a Maltese courtyard Sir Walter Scott tells me not to go. The basalt masks arrive one after the other, formed to look at oneself upside down. Employing all the techniques of an Einsteinian universe are disappointed now. The cave of red mosaic where with unobstructed vision one would see his own back. Pound met his own image coming downstairs an evening in Pisa, screaming. In sheer ooze anything he describes being his brother. Henri follows on the basis of losing the pointed sticks of the poor, and this is the subject of Bosch. But the world is matter in separation and escapes the compass. They don't make them like that, infinite worlds, dusty grapes. Thoreau is a monad, sprouting through the floor, deafening as the poor. But my joy is no longer customary, as the mud pond, obtruding in the company of fish. We do not eat rock, said Kant, for it is the knife of our individium. And like a lounger, Henri passes, talking of Giordano Bruno, creaking the olive press. The cave gives me access to the telegraphy of my synapses, and all the buxom Demeters in terra cotta I may choose. He wrote by rain, of all the small square windows of the tent. Neat as a knife to a bubble, and this is what Bosch saw. The strain is much as he has left it, all of a face, itself part of nothing in the sandstone, mirroring monads. The time is the present raging bubble. The real world drew a favorable criticism from the late quartets of Beethoven, no longer distant and hurting his head. Henri crouches like a frog in his skin, chatters like polarized light, knowing less than an arctic tavern could contain. There may be a pocket to carry an obstacle. The best imitation of a little canoe ever seen through a grist of bees. A rock is not a word. But may occupy its space? I give him my jacket as if he were on the moon. Short of Germans, they don't make them like Niobe, loose in the room. You move it up, carry the obstacle on a long string. And he awoke, colorless as light down inside a tree. Each part of the road he wrote, his notebook a pincushion drying in the warmth of the radio. In sheer weather, ghosts do not close windows. Even on flat rock, a statue is a long way. Henri runs for ten minutes on bright lawns, in sheer ooze or anything, folding his vehicular flesh from step to step. The loons drank the light as the leaves fell in bombs. A lazy talk with cigarettes. Henri seemed a shepherd, angrily & at a distance, his pushing back to the sea. Monsieur Teste lay in bed with the mask of Poe. Small trees patched up the hills, the freedom of men with breasts. The canoe had come from Holland, with candy to the lips. He lay in the olden cave, his cycling sweater pointed toward the mouth, along with Orpheus Dupin Bruno and other wiseacres. Such things of like kind bouncing from orbit to orbit, kicked around a cigarette.

The red houses unzipped, revealing the Old Stone Age, and about every string I've ever carried. Strong as a green crocodile, an American obstacle to the Boy Scouts, magic is no longer customary in the comic brevity of the world. For its part, he lifts the canoe, a drawing board with pinecone. In the seventeenth century Spinoza was painted on. Hercules was all tummy. Scott

49

stayed close to ten minutes in circles. Persephone eased the foreskin over my room. You move it up, a roofbeam into a novel. But do you make them from a kit, counterclockwise from a transparency of this century? Much of the strain was a fault of mine. I did not tell Van Gogh where to find a fresh supply. I give him some cord & he fashions a set of Wittgenstein's camp chairs, thrown grain clothing, a burst bright cavern, underlining the closing passage. The fault in your canoe, Henri, looks like a pointed stick to Van Gogh. The silence after a time is torn from him, and he stands Gauguin-straight in the sprinkler. Time is the enemy of silver, and of loons in congress. At a mighty conjunction of Riemann Bohr & Mach Henri drops his aluminum planks & steps with his left foot into the life of Julie Harris. She is Watusi and sucks lozenges, alternately tomato and campchair green. It is raining, in counterspin, the dream of rain.

II.

The present bends time and conceals a pinecone. Thereafter a wind moves on, drawn free of the sequence after a time silence is. He tore the clothes and squashed the modulor into the mud, having another white night until the supply is gone. The outline of a loon had the inclination of a name that could not be moved by congress. He gets comfortable enough to get intimate and get up cursing me. The fault in your essay is that no Indian looks at his canoe, any more than a hot coal races in circles on the surface of a white sky. Wittgenstein tossed and turned. I did not tell him where the rug had been tossed, nor how not to do it. There was no ceiling on the mine, no water in the jockstrap, no stepping on the muscles. The finest point of Victor Hugo was his temper, screaming and squealing being his defense against danger. I was about to open the newspaper to chocolates.

Charles Fourier liked dogs, enough to take a taxi for a full spin to be closer to them. Hair in a stream is better than birch bark in a mirror. The sketch runs for a full ten minutes, hours after the moon is full. Flat as a boy's canoe, the silence lifts like fire and moves on. Where do you buy those dowels that ring like bells? You portage up to the cave end, move the pins on the white wall, a ritual that ticks with insanity. The tall rampant Mondrian puts the blue cave but a short distance from his worktable, where the dodecahedrons look too fake to be fake. He figured they had to move to show intimacy. John Russell, the madman, must be blue enough by now to help the moon dance. He cowled the dead tree in convincing half-tones, and rang the bell of an Indian to further his existence. The turbulence of a figured board gives coherence to this endless room. The cubists wrote in a language officious enough for Wittgenstein without hurting his head.

Give your codpieces, every one of them, a real demonstration. I gave him every jacket he stole, without inferring a thing. It was painted on a long string. Around the bend he was, diving into the emeralds, carrying his retina on a string. Give me a board and some string and I'll give you a windmill. The Germans have come up short of Germans. I could call a German to get me some string. From my pocket on, a long string. The Germans call 1914 an obstacle or boundary. Short-wave light is terse, and German shepherds are angry. No fear of short German rule. I gave him some cord, and he trained it to kill, and it has. Then he fashioned a grid of muscles for his head, and called a second halt. At this, a pad of pictures became a language. At Lascaux oxbows form small caves in old hills. Brown houses in quagmires, slick little pointed chairs. Henri drinks down trees, and surfaces frightened. He is all patched up with the shadows and tenses with doubt. They don't make sulphur to be shaken, angrily like distant necks. In The Baltic suns are flat and three miles apart.

Grind cinnamon into the burgundy and break the sack into the ground. Canoes seem much stronger in sheer ooze. Squatting takes up much of the strain in endless room. Sit-ups in the muck, that's the best of America. The tick had left his face. Standing up, the aesthetic comes to a halt. American tennis shoes are in imitation of a Greek bike and particular illness. The mud pond is a danger to instinct. A little canoe, so neat and measurable, as a naked machine. Ovid bends over and bites Darwin, then departs, his protractors depending. Picasso was born with a large pack, and a favorable criticism from nature rather than history. Fear comes unstuck and actually overtakes him. All the wiseacres lean over his notebook, crossing themselves.

Reality is blue, over nine miles of triangle. The octopus returned to lounge in the tavern, then showed an inclination to move away. The cross is really a plumb bob. And Thoreau really sang a warm air, of his escapes from the compass, approaching the woods along the road. Thoreau went upstairs but the room was too loud and he affected a separation. The paws of the sphinx steal away from the poor. They are well run, and in time bend in silence and conceal from us the end of the cave of tension.

CAVE OF METONYMY

> "... in time (they) bend in silence
> and conceal from us the end of the
> cave of tension."
> from "Passage or Abruptness"

Hawthorne: We were speaking of Ovid bending over Darwin, of Picasso being born dead, Bergson singing a soft warm air rich in tang, a thoroughbred I might add, of Vermeer pinning down zero & Wittgenstein perhaps being prevented from washing his hands, of Cato boiling turnips, of Poussin's pounds, Gide's nipples, Gluck's water clock, Collette's pins, Van Gogh's spare room, John Hollander's soccer shirt, the holier than thou attitude of John Mcphee, Cocteau's phreatic eyes ...

Melville: Hold it! Hold it, Nate. What does "phreatic" mean?

Hawthorne: I see souls poised on the end of a pin; "Phreatic" is not in my dictionary. Maybe he meant phrenetic or freakish.

Melville: Let's stake out a section from memory, the part beginning "Who are these water striders?" up to "neat as a knife." You read it through once & then write down what you remember.

H: O.K. Here it is: "Cocteau gives me access to moonlight, to knifelight, a swell light, we itch to start the printing press so that our evenings in Pisa will be downstairs. I am your brother in an Einsteinian universe." That's really all I can remember but it's so long & really doesnt make any sense.

M: That's because he wrote on each part of the road & listened to the radio alot. He knew what he was doing, he had no time schedule. He wrote like a grist of bees for us to grind. Like cetology, this form of metonymy leaves much to thought & philosophy. What do you make of it now, Nathaniel?

H: I like a lazy talk like this with cigarettes. I'm sure "phreatic" is actually in the Oxford English Dictionary. I like looking at you with your big cigar sprouting through the floor & your voice deafening as the poor. But my joy is no longer customary because I love a long & complex sentence, not one that begins to be complex & then ends with a thud, like: "The real world drew a favorable criticism from the late quartets of Beethoven, no longer distant & hurting his head." I mean why did he have to end it on such a surrealist note.

M: That's not surrealism, Nat, that's just common sense. Since Beethoven, let's call him B for now, since B was deaf by the time he wrote the late quartets they no longer hurt his head. It's just that the end of the sentence has nothing to do with the beginning, the head hurting having no relevance to the real world's criticism & admittedly the sentence is not long.

H: The voice of reason, Herm. But look at this one: "The canoe had come from Holland, with candy to the lips."

M: A simple cut-up.

H: O.K. but where is the grace, even the gratuitousness, I could say at this point, of reason, following through, a bow to the reader & his or her mind, open to simple rationality, complex thought conveyed in fluidity of line? And it's insulting, listen to this, this is the next one: "He lay in the olden cave, his cycling sweater pointed toward the mouth, along with Orpheus Dupin Bruno & other wiseacres" Not only does he not put in the commas, he calls them wiseacres to really fuck up the sentence. And it's no accident, something weird always happens at the end. The end of each sentence. I mean, it's not as if I'm paranoid about it, is it? No, time & again we nineteenth century artists are truly fucked.

M: Never heard you wax so vehement before, Nathaniel. 1 like kicking around a sentence & a cigarette with you.

H: Good thing we both smoke.

M: Now dont brood. You know the kind of reputation you get, in fact you've already got it, Ha! The brooding methodical shy Hawthorne, contemplating the folds of Monument Mountain's Persian rug or whatever it is you said it looked like that mountain was wearing. Now really, Nathaniel, how can you accuse anybody of surrealism! You've certainly had your day, sitting around making up stories about men whose daughters wear fecal flowers in their "bosoms"—bosoms, ha! I'd never use that word. A phony closet surrealist Puritan who's obsessed with the sensual pleasures! That's what you are! Ha ha!

H: You're the one who's promoted the image of the brooder, Herman, you should talk. Pierre <u>or</u> the ambiguities, really. "And I wonder if that character is based on Melville's own life"—all the old ladies go around saying that. "Yes he lived in a dark room in New York City, just brooding cause his wife hated him," Well at least I've got my family life together & people dont have to go around speculating about what foreign religion I'll take up next. And I dont make animals the ambiguous heroes of my books. I know who's good & who's evil.

M: Now dont get rambunctious, Hawthorne, I'm quite serious. Pour me another brandy & I'll point out to you all the really lyrical lines of this fellow Coolidge.

H: Well it is a collaboration.

M: These cunts.

H: What?

M: Seriously, now listen to these: "in colors of loam & tied with string," ". . . the hippic branches of the Great Theory," "Matter is still no longer than light." Now, that's a really great one.

H: Typically, you're just picking out all the abstractions. Let's analyze this line: "A trapezius of citron from Ezra Pound in the jade stress." But before we get to that, I've been meaning to ask you what you think of this "work comes first" ethic or attitude?

M: Work comes first, yes it does. Otherwise it's like missing the train & tightening the blouse.

SOPHIA, UNA & JULIAN COME IN.

H: But Mel, he says here, "Give your codpieces, every one of them, a real demonstration." Maybe he means he likes sex more, or even anguish: "Wittgenstein tossed & turned."

M: Haw, dont be naive, you cant read into works like these. Maybe, once in a while, you'll get a direct autobiographical sentence, just mixed in like everything else that's mixed in & then you can know that that sentence is the truth. That's the nice thing about these works, they do aspire to be the truth in a way that modern language never allowed, say, you & me to come close. "A ritual that ticks with insanity," that's what he says.

H: Now, you're reading into that, when actually it says: "You portage up to the cave end, move the pins on the white wall, a ritual that ticks with insanity." What does that ever mean? What pins? I must admit the preceding sentence is a knockout for a short one: "Where do you buy those dowels that ring like bells?" All modern life, but still assonant. I think he's got something there.

M: Dont be so sociological. I'll begin to think I'm in a motel room. You're forgetting the important points: the repetition of cadences, are these works autobiographical?, what does the syntax have to do with the meaning or the world?, can we have a good modern writer?, etc. The pins are obviously the ones you use for caving & stress is a caving word too, or a geological one.

H: Not in my dictionary.

M: You're very dependent on the authorities for someone who's become a scandal.

H: I wish you didnt know everything that's ever happened to me like that.

56

M: Why shouldnt I? We're contemporaries & we've opened our lives up to the goddamned public for whatever it's worth by putting our fucking names & faces out in the open. You jackass you've even had your portrait done a thousand times so that everybody & his mother can think your faggot eyes follow them all around the room when they feel corrupted enough to stare at your oily likeness.

Sophia: I feel that when Coolidge says, for instance, "The cubists wrote in a language officious enough for Wittgenstein without hurting his head," we have a problem to solve, if we are willing & interested enough to deal with it at all, which of course I at the least always am. Now, first of all, there's the flow of the language which the sentence takes quite beautifully & seriously from beginning to middle, which I would estimate to be after the word "enough", to its own beautiful & complex ending, almost something I would like to hang in the hall. Here we suddenly bring in Wittgenstein, to my great delight, confuse him with Beethoven who was deaf when he wrote the last quartets. For me, the previous thought, "no longer distant" in relation to Beethoven, is the key. That is, the cubists' language is, if you will forgive me, a link, in this poet's mind, whether unconscious or no, between the grand qualities of the music of the master & modern life in its rare forms, with Wittgenstein, the great progenitor of all real interpretation, scientific and literary, as the fine & generous restorer here of the famous "endless room" referred to in the work. Wittgenstein has in fact created the endless room, it is his idea & not, if you may excuse an extension of this reading further, the idea or ideas of the writer or writers. Why they steal so much is beyond my moral comprehension. Wittgenstein in fact formulated the endless room in no. 59A of PHILOSOPHICAL INVESTIGATIONS. These writers that you pore over so deeply, Herman & Nathaniel, are just humans forced to open the newspaper to chocolates. And so to bed.

H: Ah, Sophia, you are too generous.

M: Well said, Sophia.

Una: Igloo! Igloo!

Julian: What ho? What do you say, Oony?

Sophia: Children, hush. And leave the more abstruse definitions to those who will have their entire adulthoods caught up in that disease of the senses. And remember that God has endowed us with a finer sense of what is to be than these moderns acknowledge, they who study, willy-nilly, insensibility. Yet we still live, we who have studied the trapezoid birth of these more unparallel yet necessary apparati of today's intellectual life. Yes, letters will die before the unwieldy sentence regains its form. And so, goodnight.

H: Sophia really had a point there.

M: As always, as always.

A KNOCK AT THE DOOR. HAWTHORNE ADMITS THE MIDNIGHT GUESTS.

Louis Malle: Hello!

Paul: Hello!

Melville: Ah, we were discussing Coolidge in his cave collaboration with that tart Mayer.

LM: So, have you discussed the sentence: "Mondrian puts the blue cave but a short distance from his worktable, where the dodecahedrons look too fake to be fake?"

M: Which one?

H: You mean the sentence followed by: "He figured they had to move to show intimacy?"

LM: Yes, that's it. The most daring sentence in modern literature, so far. Except of course, I find it hard to keep up with their magazines coming out so irregularly & so much of who's published where & when depending on mood & fraternity. It's so cooled down, so un-barbarous.

H: Yes, but they do write alot, I mean they produce alot of good writing, if you can follow them & it.

M: Hawthorne here has just had a lesson in integrity.

H: Herman, I would appreciate your not advertising my inadequacies to every passing stranger.

M: Actually, Mr. Nathaniel Everyman Has-Thorn, I praise you to the skies when you arent around.

H: Well, hot noogies, now that Sophia's gone to bed. So what do you think of these new pinecones, the collaborationists, Paul?

Paul: Good work, good work. They're going in the right direction, yet . . .

H: Yet?

P: Well Hawthorne, I enjoy you yet I know I remain an enigma to you because I'm closer to the real world . . .

H: Paul, please dont flaunt your amazing youth & vitality & independence & Yankee individualism. We arent talking about you, though I must say, for stupid Herman's edification, that your idea of the page is a totally integral one & you are certainly more inspiring, for a young person, than these people who just string ideas together, even words, without generosity to the rational reader & besides, you know how to . . .

LM: You mean like: "Reality is blue, over nine miles of triangle. The octopus returned . . . ?"

P: Coolidge prefers the bath to nature. Very few adjectives.

M: Now, you see Nathaniel, there's a real down-to-earth cirrus cloud, I mean, criticism, none of that soul-in-your-shoe phantasy about German Shepherds meaning sado-masochistic restraint, tying up, that sort of thing.

P: Now you're really way off the mark.

H: Wait a second Herman, I think you've had too much brandy.

LM: The resolution of all this is really in the hand. If only all of you guys had taken a turn writing your own film scripts.

H: Dont you flaunt your modernity, Luis.

M: Now where you get off calling him "Luis" I'll never know, just because you been to Rome & even that's past history.

H: I didnt say "Luis" I said "Loo-ie" as in "Henri." Give Paul some of your famous brand-ee.

M: From my pocket on, I swear I shall never understand the boyscout mind of Nathaniel Hawthorne.

H: Herman, infants could teach you what a simple sentence is.

LM: Now wait a minute, you two great guys cant get into such a mess about what a simple person like Clark Coolidge means. He's direct enough, he likes the movies.

P: And learns much from them.

M: Now what do you mean by that, Paul? I thought you were making sense & here you go defending the wrong thing.

P: What's the wrong thing? Just because you think I'm down-to-earth doesnt mean I agree with you.

M: But you're supposed to tell Hawthorne what's going on, he's up a tree.

H: I'm no further up a tree than you were when you thought a pizza might help your house out.

M: Now you're really getting plain, a fine friendship this turned out to be. And I told that reporter I was in love with you.

H: What? Well if you didnt insist on drinking so much we might have a coherent discussion, just the four of us, instead of letting literature fly to the winds.

M: Fly to the winds, typical. Eat your heart out Hawthorne, you'll never be as good as Coolidge cause you just arent as smart.

H: Smart, ha! He's just trying to imitate Mabel Mercer & that's where he's at.

M: Never knew you'd heard of her.

H: I'll put her on the record player, sure.

LM: Please do.

Mabel Mercer sings:
    Danger I'll eat your heart out
    Tall as a waterboy's portage end
    And boy, you are tall as
    A blue dodecahedron move of Mondrian's
    He steals south around my muscles
    Approaches up in American history

    Man you gotta see him
    Man you gotta see him
    Its bends conceal us

Such a cigarette, freedom of men
Rather than history
Oh man you gotta see him grind cinnamon
You gotta see the big mud pond
Rather than history
You gotta see the Germans

I gave him some cord but he
fashioned a grid of muscles for me
He called it language, just
Small caves in old hills
The bites so neat we tore the clothes
& he's cursing me in a fashion
Of a cavern

It's raining & man you gotta see him
The dream of rain you gotta see him in
Counterspin, I find the falling danger
I'll eat your heart out
taller than a boy scout
We steal the south bend around
My American history sound

I wake up as Rilke said
Man, my tree heart is dead
But man you gotta see
Coolidge drinkin tea
You gotta fit your fuckin shoe
To the Great Theory
He aint bleary
He's close to the cities
It's the nitty-gritties
That gave us Stan Kenton

So declare your pennies
Cause they put a dent in

My blue jeans canoe
Its bends conceal us
And we sneak up the river, honey, just its
   bends annihilate
So Doctor Hegel can try a late
Appearance, lovers of danger
Gotta stay flat in our shoes
Lovers of danger
We seal up our caves with canoes

SAM & FLOYD, PURGATORY AGAIN

Beckett: Well, what think you, Floyd, of these meanders?

Collins: I never read much, printed sheets, that is, 'ceptin' the labels on kerosene
cans in my work. Heard voices sometimes.

B: There's Melville, see, who wished to bring all the world to himself, & Mayer who
wanted all of herself to the world. Or is that too neat an edge?

C: It's true, the cave is rough enough to hold a rock edge and then black air.

B: Disgusting. It's either all the connections or none. Must we always have it either
way? Maybe best I should join you over that cold can of beans in the darkness.

C: You could do worse. These people who sit and scribble . . . I'd like to plunk
'em down sudden like, say in the Lost Passage with no lights. See who or what
emerges.

B: Fairly extreme, Floyd. But maybe no more so than in my cubicle with the
single window looking out on nothing, the empty page in my head, always the
sharpened pencil waiting for . . .

C: One of my prime rules: never wait. Move on if you find yourself lacking a
direction. You'll find yourself in one, and sometimes enough of a pickle. After all
I finally ended up . . .

B: Christ, I know well enough. I've always tried to end each sentence carefully and
doubtless, but the final twist of syntax fitted out with a period's never enough.
I've never been able to end anything. My horror, not a sentence that ever ends.

C: Same with caves, Sam. They sometimes pinch you but never quite close. Fair
maddening. Speechless. Caves at least give you that. Rule Two: always go alone.
But I've spoken more since I've been here with you than I reckon I did in the
whole of my life down there.

B: They always said I did tend to draw people out. But that's one of the least of
my failings. No wonder I was never able to finish my books, always ending by
starting another one. But what of this Coolidge, seems he landed in a grotto
himself a time or two. God knows why. He certainly didn't. Probably couldn't
help himself once he'd started.

C: Probably wanted to shut his mouth and strain his eyes instead. Caves are
lighthouses for the blind. From what you say about his books he was always

getting lost off the main passage, and that's the nature of a cave gets you to pondering. There's surely no one way.

B: That's what I always tried to tell Joyce. Poor soul, always thought himself stuck in the thoroughfare. Of course, he was quite the hot one for a crack. But then cracks do lead us?

C: Sometimes I used to hear voices calling me down there. Sometimes they'd tell me which way to go. But if they called on me to wait up for 'em then I knew I was fucked.

B: My voices always seem to be trying to tell me where I am, or worse, where I've been. Either way they keep me from finishing. Maybe I should pay more attention to Mayer, bringing every flick of herself up to the moment each time. She gets a momentum that way I wish I could build. But I seem caught in the reverse, the future a baffle of ice I slip from, one step forward makes two steps back.

C: Got trapped below a mud slope one day, until I hit on the idea of embedding slabs in it far enough up till I got a handhold. Took me most of a day but I got out. Reminds me a bit of what you say about that fellow Coolidge, how he escaped from one of his books. Nothing but jump-offs and clambers, this life.

B: So called. You never trusted what took place in the open air. Rather trust to the still solids, seeming still that is.

C: Nothing to do with Nature, that one. Just my own fault.

B: Ha, and there's Mayer titling her writing Agoraphobia. And Coolidge dreaming of a kind of music that sets like painting. They think they'll have an end of it, but they've got another thing coming.

C: Sam, you've really got an itch 'bout endings, maybe 'cause you ain't even dead and buried. But look at me. That measly leetle boulder put a finish to me, along with all them strangers mucking around taking so long to start anything practical, and here I am jawing with the likes of you still and have to watch them fellers stumbling on my links. If this is an "ending" to anything I'd like you to tell me just how.

B: Yes. It's just as I feared. I always wanted what there's absolutely none of. See that chair? That's where I've taken to sitting to watch one sunset after another. Abysmal!

C: Listen, Sam, beyond that wall is a whole other system. I always knew it and sometime I even found it. Quite a few them fellers haven't even found yet.

B: I even have to sit and watch Coolidge & Mayer writing further and more endless books! And it seems they haven't even finished with Melville and Hawthorne! At least my writing's getting shorter. Each time . . .

C: All illusion, Sam. Like some stalactites I've seen, condensations of whole mountains of lime.

B: I didn't know you knew such terms as "condensation", Floyd.

C: See, that's the thing about being dead. It's <u>all</u> here at once. Lacking time, nothing is hidden. Not a wall can hold my vision, now it's too late . . .

B: Sounds like living in a dictionary. And I know a little of that.

C: One of us is waiting and one of us isn't.

B: Ha! Try and tell them that. Or any of this. Now, how about telling one more story about the Lost Passage. And turn out the light. That way your sentences get longer.

CLARK AND BERNADETTE IN THE PARADISE OF THE LAST PASSAGE

B: How come Clark we keep putting words whatever they are
into each other's mouths? It's just like, forgive me,
thinking my matches are "korectype" or my beer ink.

C: It's not mouths it's more like mice or dialogues; in this
form we can't exactly take such quick turns turning as the
books fall into . . .

B: Ice leaves? Ice cream cones? Like the peak of a volcano
or a bloodsucking conenose, like a wedge of something or
the woody stiff fruit of a certain tree, like sucking the
blood of books . . . oh I can't go on . . . as we do . . .

C: Some can go on; some do not. This has gone on too long.

B: I know not much lives in caves especially below the Circle.

C: <u>Inside</u> the Circle. Your circle?

B: Your circle, Scott's, whose?

C: Do you want to lose . . .

B: Let's do a couplet or a quatrain . . .

C: For those who read backwards. What exactly was your fear
of entering the cave? What did happen?

B: We're older now than at the beginning of this book
Do we actually need to stun that image with another look?

C: Have you ever seen the movie Ed took of the walk through Eldon's?
Remember the chowder and brandy, why if we remember all hell then's . . .

B: Forgiveness in this Proustian shared paradise's chance
Of remembering caving so lost together for a while

C: This book fuller of stuff in its middle than each end's silly dance
Of holy silly memory's craving to be dead or friendly in some style

B: You said it!

C: Can't we ever end it!

B: Holier than you I must run through the free caves for something!

C: Hottest something is the ice that blends our drinks to nothing!

B: I wish to bring each situating climb up to the moment or fall!

C: I know this narrow escarpment today becomes our love of all!

B: All this stuff and everything,

C: Moment's nothing still for the new but something.

B: I gave you the last word.

C: And that's the last I heard.

Let's just stop, but still we'll have to wait
for something proves the next lost thing to last
like caves words leave a hollow in our past
we bet on hopes our absence sets in state

Of memory finance passages stay best
they go but leading play out rates to find
that cleavable arrangement in the mind
of one by two that follows all the rest

This stint might turn out charts for our compartment
traps that stick more lasting than our blood
that day struck more from remnants thin of mood
our book made full in faulting more than statement

Hear you not abandon calling you?
that not a closure turned will stand abating
these portages we'll leave in place of waiting
the passages thought left we'll call them through